"Teenagers need to be able to set and achieve goals, but their executive functioning often isn't fully developed. Drawing on the latest neuroscience, Lara Honos-Webb provides a road map for mastering these skills—which will set up teens for success not only in high school, but throughout their lives."

> —**Daniel H. Pink**, author of *When* and *Drive*

"Lara Honos-Webb has done it again. With *6 Super Skills for Executive Functioning*, she has created a road map for teens and their parents to improve executive function and motivation to change related maladaptive habits—and to do so in a positive (re)frame. Her deep knowledge and experience working successfully with teens who have executive function issues is demonstrated in each suggestion she offers."

> —**Robin S. Rosenberg, PhD, ABPP**, CEO and founder of
> Live in Their World; adjunct clinical faculty at University
> of California, San Francisco; and coauthor of *Abnormal
> Psychology* and *Introducing Psychology*

"'How can I envision, set, and achieve my goals in life?' Lara Honos-Webb breaks down this question for teens and young adults in a simple, step-by-step manner that is easy to follow for any reader. This book teaches big dreamers how to think S.M.A.R.T, deal with life's challenges, and achieve ambitions with grit."

> —**Grace Friedman,** advocate, speaker, founder of
> www.addyteen.com, and coauthor of *Winning with ADHD*

"Another informative and inspiring book by Lara Honos-Webb. This book is full of action-oriented tools that guide teenagers to learn the skills they need to stay focused, set goals, manage stress, stop negative thinking habits, and ultimately chart a course of positive thinking. Lara writes with compassion, acceptance, and optimism—as she encourages teenagers to shift their mind-set, and move to a place of self-empowerment."

—**Robin Goldstein, PhD**, instructor of child and
adolescent psychology at University of Maryland,
Baltimore County (UMBC)

"While reading Lara Honos-Webb's clear and encouraging guide, my thoughts turned to the many people who go through life never believing in their own competence. She wants each teen to know that their minds can practice and grow important skills they might believe are impossible. She offers not only hope, but reassurance that they can build self-discipline and discover its gift—the freedom to choose."

—**Margaret Robinson Rutherford, PhD**, clinical psychologist,
and author of *Perfectly Hidden Depression*

"A great continuation of *BRAIN HACKS*. Lara Honos-Webb is the best specialist in executive functions for all inhabitants of the neurodiversity planet: neurotypicals and neurodivergents. In these times of 'electronality,' where virtuality re-signifies our life, we must relearn how to develop each mind into the gift that it must become. *6 Super Skills for Executive Functioning* teaches us how."

—**Ernesto Reaño**, psychologist, linguist,
and author of *The Return to the Village*

"Lara Honos-Webb has created a beautiful guide to self-mastery for youth who are struggling with executive function challenges that is accessible and straightforward. Backed by the latest research, it is chock-full of helpful tips to create positive shifts in mind-set that will empower any youth who practices these skills. This is definitely on my list of favorites to share with the neurodiverse kids I work with, and their parents."

—**Shawn V. Giammattei, PhD**, professor of clinical psychology at Alliant International University, and founder and director of the Gender Health Training Institute and Quest Family Therapy

"Once again, Lara Honos-Webb has brilliantly put together an actionable and inspiring book for those with attention deficit/hyperactivity disorder (ADHD)—this time written to teens. The 'super skills' she shares in this book, synthesized through years of her own clinical research, are transformative tools that will be a true gift to each reader who applies them. The book's content is well researched and peppered with illustrative stories to make it an enjoyable and accessible read."

—**Mary Illions Wilde, MD**, integrative pediatrician, and owner of Imagine Pediatrics Behavioral Health and Wellness

"As a person with ADHD, I wish I had this book as a teenager. Lara Honos-Webb combines real science and real talk to help us understand our minds and achieve our goals. Most importantly, this book provides a road map for self-discovery—helping teens tune into their gifts, identify their strengths, and build confidence along the way."

—**Margaux Joffe**, founder of Kaleidoscope Society for women with ADHD, and corporate social responsibility leader

the *instant* help
solutions series

Young people today need mental health resources more than ever. That's why New Harbinger created the **Instant Help Solutions Series** especially for teens. Written by leading psychologists, physicians, and professionals, these evidence-based self-help books offer practical tips and strategies for dealing with a variety of mental health issues and life challenges teens face, such as depression, anxiety, bullying, eating disorders, trauma, and self-esteem problems.

Studies have shown that young people who learn healthy coping skills early on are better able to navigate problems later in life. Engaging and easy-to-use, these books provide teens with the tools they need to thrive—at home, at school, and on into adulthood.

This series is part of the **New Harbinger Instant Help Books** imprint, founded by renowned child psychologist Lawrence Shapiro. For a complete list of books in this series, visit newharbinger.com.

6 super skills

for executive functioning

tools to help teens improve
focus, stay organized
& reach their goals

LARA HONOS-WEBB, PhD

Instant Help Books
An Imprint of New Harbinger Publications, Inc.

Publisher's Note

This publication is designed to provide accurate and authoritative information in regard to the subject matter covered. It is sold with the understanding that the publisher is not engaged in rendering psychological, financial, legal, or other professional services. If expert assistance or counseling is needed, the services of a competent professional should be sought.

Distributed in Canada by Raincoast Books

Copyright © 2020 by Lara Honos-Webb
        New Harbinger Publications, Inc.
        5674 Shattuck Avenue
        Oakland, CA 94609
        www.newharbinger.com

Cover design by Amy Shoup; Acquired by Tesilya Hanauer; Edited by Karen Schader

Library of Congress Cataloging-in-Publication Data

Names: Honos-Webb, Lara, author. | Brown, Neil D, author.
Title: Six super skills for executive functioning : tools to help teens improve focus, stay organized, and reach their goals / Lara Honos-Webb, Neil D Brown.
Other titles: 6 super skills for executive functioning
Description: Oakland : New Harbinger Publications, 2020. | Includes bibliographical references.
Identifiers: LCCN 2020019873 (print) | LCCN 2020019874 (ebook) | ISBN 9781684035335 (trade paperback) | ISBN 9781684035342 (pdf) | ISBN 9781684035359 (epub)
Subjects: LCSH: Teenagers--Time management--Juvenile literature. | Study skills--Juvenile literature. | Attention--Juvenile literature.
Classification: LCC BF637.T5 H66 2020 (print) | LCC BF637.T5 (ebook) | DDC 155.5/19--dc23
LC record available at https://lccn.loc.gov/2020019873
LC ebook record available at https://lccn.loc.gov/2020019874

Printed in the United States of America

22   21   20

10 9 8 7 6 5 4 3 2 1   First Printing

This book is dedicated to my two teens who wouldn't want to have their names in their embarrassing mom's book. I hope someday you will read this and know it's a love letter to both of you.

Contents

Foreword

The challenges of being a teenager and raising a teenager are well known. Parents struggle with getting their teenagers to manage responsibilities and stay out of trouble. Teenagers find themselves buried by the many responsibilities they face while seeking social acceptance and independence. Teens often feel that what's being asked of them is beyond them. Many of the youth I've worked with, although intellectually capable or even gifted, are neurologically challenged to succeed in a classroom environment. Differences such as ADHD, autism spectrum disorder, or dyslexia put teens and their parents at odds, often building control battles that invite youth resistance and frustrate and leave parents in a state of burnout. Even without a diagnosable condition, youth grow in different ways and at different rates, and simply lacking maturation in an area will frustrate many youth and their families.

As a family therapist who works with teenagers, I've helped countless families end their control battles and align adolescent and parental efforts for teenagers to grow, mature, and experience happiness and success along the way. And while I have done my best to help young people develop healthy self-valuing habits and do their best, the therapeutic community, myself included, has been short on tools to offer teenagers to get them past their stuck spots. Procrastination, low motivation, low interest, poor organization, and ubiquitous connected device distraction are just some of the challenges that teenagers and their parents, as well as therapists and educators who want to help them, are facing.

For too long, these issues have been used to blame and label teenagers in ways that add to their feelings of frustration, inadequacy, and futility. Now in her groundbreaking new book, Dr. Honos-Webb utilizes the emerging knowledge of adolescent neural development and provides a road map for teens to grow and develop their executive function skills. She takes the mystery out of procrastination, fear of failure, low motivation, low self-confidence, and underperformance and brings youth the hope, optimism, and skills that lead to both immediate relief and improvement, as well as lasting growth to serve a lifetime.

Honos-Webb does not talk down to teenagers; she doesn't simply give personal advice. Rather, she brings real science and cites studies and research to help them understand the roots of their behavior as well as evidence-based ways to change. With her six super skills, she brings a powerful and engaging way for teenagers to build their executive functioning. Each of the skills improves several areas of the five executive functions: planning and organization, focus, flexible thinking, emotion regulation, and impulse control. As adolescents apply these skills, they improve their own neurological development. Just as running more will make them faster, applying Honos-Webb's super skills will build brain strength, literally creating neural pathways that make work easier.

Throughout the book and in each of the six super skills, Honos-Webb offers ways to replace negative self-talk with positive self-talk. This theme of seeing oneself in a positive light begins with the first super skill, finding gifts, and is reinforced throughout the book. Honos-Webb uses this positive view of self, along with science-based actionable solutions to common and normal challenges, and invites and challenges youth to utilize these skills for self-empowerment, take charge of their lives, and set and accomplish personal goals. The result is a book that will change lives.

As a child enters middle school and their teen years, responsible parents and educators prepare them with sex education, explaining the maturational transformation their bodies are going through. *Six Super Skills for Executive Functioning* provides that same vital education to teens and their parents in the area of neurological transformation. As middle schoolers experience the normal struggles of managing their work, behaviors, and emotions, this book that will help them and their parents understand and address the challenges.

Six Super Skills will benefit not only young teen; it is also a perfect resource for young adults looking for ways to improve their college performance. For teenagers of any age experiencing mild to serious problems in their functioning, *Six Super Skills* offers powerful tools to reclaim their lives.

It's not a book to read and put on the shelf when you're done. It's a book to read, reread, mark up, consult with, and put into action. This is not a book to hand a teenager and walk away. This book will help not only teenagers but also the parents, therapists, and educators working to guide them toward success. It provides a long needed road map they can use together to address problems and maximize potential.

—Neil Brown,
author of *Ending the Parent–Teen Control Battle*

Introduction

We can all get caught in the trap of comparing our darkest moments to others' greatest wins. We are surrounded by social media images of the happiest, most filtered, flattering, proudest moments of those in our social circle. The path to being happy in a world that offers many reasons for dissatisfaction is to choose what you focus on. That choice will determine your emotions.

One teen could take a vacation to Hawaii and sulk about their parents taking their phone away. Another person could be sidelined from soccer season due to an injury and redirect their attention to their childhood passion of journaling and feel that their world has opened up. You can see from the contrast that you can choose your reaction to life events.

This book is a guide to self-mastery. The ability to control your thoughts and feelings and actions will greatly impact your mental health and also your ability to get your goals. It is the discipline to get those goals that gives you the liberty to go where you want to go. So instead of thinking of discipline as limiting your freedom, see that it is discipline that gives you a license to choose. You, like most teens, want to be independent, to govern your own life, and the most straight forward path to that is through self-command. Research shows that self-discipline predicts your grades twice as much as IQ (Duckworth and Seligman 2005). There's just one catch for you—your brain has not completely finished developing.

Imagine being in a home where every week there were new contractors doing construction on three different projects while you were trying to live there. That's what it's like to be a teenager. Your hormones are changing, your body is changing, and so is your brain.

This book is about *executive functioning*—the ability to plan, take action rather than procrastinate, consider multiple possibilities to help you solve problems, and stay focused. Executive functioning involves your "will," defined as determination, insistence, persistence, or willfulness. Synonyms for "will" include power, resolve, intention, decisiveness, and self-restraint.

The term "executive function" is an umbrella term that includes many interrelated functions that allow you to control your thoughts, feelings, and behavior. You will learn about the five core components of executive functioning:

- attention
- planning
- flexible thinking
- emotion regulation
- impulse control

Your executive functioning is still under construction, and it will likely be fully developed closer to age twenty-five.

The good news is that the earlier you start taking charge of your thoughts, the more you are strengthening control over your brain. Neuropsychologists talk about neural pathways that strengthen the more you use them and diminish the less you use them; this capacity is called *neuroplasticity* and is often summed up as "the neurons that fire together wire together." The more you use the six super skills covered in this book to build executive functioning, the easier these will become. The less you give in to procrastination and negative thoughts, the weaker these negative aspects will be.

This book will throw dozens of tools at you. Some of these tools will work for you, and some may not. If you find a handful of tools that work for you, you can begin to see progress, which itself will motivate you.

Crisis in Cognition

Not only are teens challenged by having executive functioning that is still a work in progress, but also experts are warning that adults are facing a crisis in cognition caused by the ever-present, never-ending distraction of technology, especially our smartphones (Gazzaley 2018). Research shows that having a phone present even if you aren't using it reduces cognitive capacity (Ward et al. 2017).

Cognition means the thinking process itself. Multitasking is damaging to cognition; it has been found to increase stress and create cognitive losses more serious than does smoking weed (Levitin 2015). The crisis of cognition is more of a challenge for teens because of the close scrutiny you're under in every class, on every sports field, and at home. Because your brain is still developing, you are more likely to take missteps that are met with criticism, correction, or consequences. I expect that you wish the well-meaning adults in your life could have X-ray vision and see all the construction going on in your brain and body, how hard you are trying, and at times how hard you are on yourself trying to juggle high standards, close monitoring, and fear of failure.

Why are we in a crisis now? Think of a special occasion when you went to a brunch buffet. There may have been hundreds of options, including your favorite breakfast and lunch items, from pancakes and bacon to prime rib and chocolate-covered strawberries. In this metaphor, eating carrot sticks is like finding focus. They get lost in all the more attractive options. When it comes to entertainment, social connections, and gaming, there are many more distractions than you could ever consume. And they are addictive.

Ten years ago, the term "executive functioning" was mostly used by neuropsychologists. But in part because of the crisis of cognition created by technology, it is now a mainstream word.

Self-Discovery

I hope this book can become a guide for you to chart a path from goal setting to goal getting. This process goes beyond self-help to self-discovery, the essential value of the lifelong process of gaining self-knowledge through a loving curiosity about this creature—your essential you—that you are the caretaker of. While the skills you learn are backed by science, connecting to your essential self is the poetry of your soul. Your dreams, imagination, and desires can be your most potent guides.

My second hope for you is that even if you take away only one or two new habits from this book, over the course of your lifetime you will enjoy seeing your dreams come true. If you had a penny and doubled it every day for thirty days, how much money do you think you would have? The answer is $5,368,709.12! If you make small investments in yourself every day and build on those, incredible things can happen.

I wish I could tell you this is simple and easy. The truth is that it takes work. You won't change overnight, but you will be constantly evolving. Here's the good news: you are the one who benefits from all the work. Think about the penny that doubled every day to make more than 5 million dollars in one month. Remember, doing the work gives you more freedom to get what you want and ultimately to be independent.

Be an Encourager

I'm certain that you sometimes get the message that it's all about competition, that you have to be better than someone else. Let's switch that around and believe that we have to be our best so our contribution can make another person a better person. Your contribution can make a better world, and the other person's contribution will also make a better world. You want other people to get their goals too. They will help create a better world for you and your loved ones to live in. Be an encourager, to yourself and to others.

How to Read This Book

As you go through this book, scan a few pages, identify your questions, reread to try to answer those questions—and be patient. An important point to remember is that each executive function skill is related to the others; it will take the whole book to get a very clear picture of that. It's like studying anatomy: you'll learn each term as you study it, but the overall interrelations will begin to take shape only after repetition. As you dig deeper in each chapter, the relationship between super skills and the executive functions will slowly become more and more clear.

A journal can help you navigate through this book, so you can see the progress you make as you follow each step. You can also use Notes on an iPhone or Microsoft OneNotes on an Android. You can create a folder for this book where you will jot down answers to questions and responses to guided exercises.

Tell Yourself

Take a deep breath, and try to have fun with this. It will pay off! Tell yourself, *Listen, you are far more capable than you ever thought, let alone dreamed of. You are a champ; you got this. Go get 'em!*

You're the owner of your brain. But it goes deeper than that; you're the owner of the "you." There isn't another you. There never has been and never will be. Relish that. Cherish it. Use it as motivation to become whatever you want to become.

CHAPTER 1

Goal Getting

Our goals can only be reached through a vehicle of a plan, in which we must fervently believe, and upon which we must vigorously act. There is no other route to success.

—Pablo Picasso

Let me guess. A parent handed you this book. And that only proves how embarrassing and clueless they really are (☺). Or maybe it was a school counselor or therapist who recommended you learn more about executive functioning. Perhaps the word "executive" reminds you of the CEO of a company, and you are wondering what it has to do with you. One way to think of executive functioning is being the boss of your brain, making decisions that help you get your goals. Improving your executive functioning simply means increasing your ability to set goals and get goals.

As we review the basics in this chapter, remember that goal getting is the outcome of executive functioning and super skills. It's important to keep at the top of your mind the benefits of getting your goals. Think of a time when you achieved a goal. It may have been running the mile in eight minutes for PE class or getting a 5 on your AP Biology test. You likely felt a happy fullness and a sense of contentment and completion. The harder you worked for it, the greater the joy.

Each goal you achieve gives you a sense of confidence to begin the cycle for setting a new goal. You can savor that feeling, and even say to yourself, *I'm living the dream come true* when you achieve a goal. Even just the act of planning a new goal can make you feel hopeful, challenged, and ambitious. One of my mottos is "Do hard things with low stakes so you can do hard things when the stakes are high." Even small goals will increase your capacity to do hard things that will serve your highest-stake goals.

This book will give you a guide for how to be an ambitious teen. Sometimes people are shy to call themselves ambitious—maybe they won't live up to all their ambition and will then feel silly. Some teens don't think it's cool to be ambitious, but as you build confidence you won't worry so much about what other people think, or play small to please someone else.

Are You Tied Too Tightly to Your Phone?

You may have a smartphone, a tablet, a computer connected to the internet, a TV with multiple streaming services, a gaming console. Through these devices, you have access to social media, powerful search engines, entertainment, news—in short, endless distractions. Screen time is associated with harmful health outcomes, including depressive symptoms and quality of life (Stiglic and Viner 2019). About 25 percent of children and teens show a pattern of smartphone use that looks like an addiction labeled as "problematic smartphone use." This pattern of use predicts depression, anxiety, stress, and poor sleep (Sohn et al. 2019).

How many times a day do you think you touch your phone? Pause here and make a guess.

If you are like a typical American, you touch your phone eighty times a day—that is, every twelve minutes (SWNS 2017). Research has shown that just the presence of your phone drains your brain's ability to pay attention (Ward et al. 2017).

Many experts are warning of a cognition crisis that is only getting worse. In a 2018 article, Dr. Adam Gazzaley warns that "our constant engagement with technology interferes with the pursuit of other behaviors critical for maintaining a healthy mind, such as nature exposure, physical movement, face-to-face contact, and restorative sleep." He continues: "Its negative influence on empathy, compassion, cooperation, and social bonding are just beginning to be understood."

The prime suspect in this cognition crisis is that phone in your hands. Make no mistake, that phone can increase productivity—that's why it was made! You can have a calendar, some artificial intelligence capability to deliver reminders, and freedom from having to remember people's phone numbers because your contacts are right on the phone.

A big drawback of that phone is the effect of spending so much time on the entertainment it offers you. You can stream TV shows and movies, watch YouTube all day, play video games, and spend hours on Instagram and Snapchat. Even kids who are more academic than social can get lost in Reddit feeds, special interest news sites, or strategy-based video games, such as *Hearthstone*. The phone can become a major distraction from staying on target with your goals.

The challenge for you will be to maximize the capacity for a phone to take over some specific tasks that require focused attention, such as remembering phone numbers, accessing dates of important events, and programming reminders of tests and homework assignments.

You will also have to find ways to limit your use of the endless entertainment of movies, TV shows, video games, social media, and more. Apple has introduced screen time monitoring that provides feedback about how much time you are spending on specific apps and allows you to limit access to those same apps. The screen time function is not enough. You will also need to learn to remind yourself of what you are missing out on that could enhance your life, as you spend more than two or three hours on your phone a day. For example, that time on Snapchat could be replacing time exercising, socializing face-to-face, or planning the week ahead.

This book will help you strengthen your ability to manage your attention, including your phone, and give you ideas for how to use the smartphone effectively to take over direct attention tasks and increase your productivity.

Positive Self-Talk

Ask yourself, *What are the benefits of this time on technology? What am I missing out on by spending time on technology now?*

The Big Five Components of Executive Functioning

In order to achieve your goals, you will need to strengthen your (1) attention, (2) planning, (3) flexible thinking, (4) emotion regulation, and (5) impulse control. Like playing the piano or perfecting your baseball pitch, practice in one area will increase your skill level in all these areas.

Attention

Have you noticed that sometimes you can easily pay attention and other times you just can't get yourself to stay tuned in? Our attention is often driven by motivation and interest. If you are interested in math but not biology, you will find it easier to pay attention in math class and harder in biology class. There is a great deal of research on what you can do to increase your attention—even toward things you don't find all that interesting—and what the major disrupters of attention are. Chapter 7 will give you an overview of what you can do to help your attention and what harms it.

Planning

Goal setting is the most important element of planning. You can practice setting daily, weekly, monthly, and yearly goals to build your capacity to take charge of where you're going in your life. If you have a goal to spend a semester abroad when you go away to college, you will more likely get that goal if you start planning now. You might plan to get good grades in Spanish and to save up money so you can help pay for the costs. When you think this far ahead, you can start looking for part-time jobs. If you want to get those good grades in Spanish, you have to make sure you have a command center for your schoolwork. Do you know where your books and folders are? Do you have index cards so you can make flash cards? Should you download the app Duo Lingo, which can make review fast and easy? Should you schedule chunks of time to drill yourself on vocabulary? Once you have a goal, you need a strategy to help with planning.

Flexible Thinking

Being a teen means you have a lot to figure out. You often have to try a lot of things out to get clear about what you really want in life and what's actually going to work. For example, you may think that if you don't get all As you will never be successful. This thought may create intense anxiety that makes it even harder to pay attention. You can set a goal to get all As, and also use flexible thinking to manage your anxiety about what's at stake if you don't get all As. You can use flexible thinking so that you can feel confident in yourself and your future even if you don't get all your goals.

Emotion Regulation

As you work toward your goals, it's important to avoid the pitfalls of too much anxiety and getting so discouraged after setbacks that you fail to bounce back. You can also get derailed from your goals by emotional upsets caused by drama in your friendships, feeling left out, teachers who are unfair, parents who don't understand, and much more. Some teens try to regulate their emotions through bad habits, numbing themselves with video games, unhealthy food, alcohol, or drugs. If you learn how you can improve your own mood, how to use emotions as signals to yourself from yourself about yourself, you will protect yourself from using technology, food, or substances to try to feel good or numb intense feelings.

Impulse Control

Impulsiveness is acting before thinking. In order to achieve your goals, you need to avoid checking your phone every twelve minutes or saying yes to every invitation to get frozen yogurt. One of the most important tools for managing impulsiveness is to practice pausing before acting; for example, if you feel the urge to play an addictive video game, you can tell yourself, *Not now. I can always play later.*

This tool is also called delayed gratification. The longer you can delay gratification, the more time you can devote to working toward your goals by planning, engaging in healthy pleasures that regulate your mood, and getting started on what you need to do. One way to practice being more deliberate about your choices is to simply start asking yourself what the benefits and costs of a certain action are. Doing this can increase your ability to stay on target with goal-directed activities, rather than giving in to distracting impulses.

The Six Super Skills

This book will show you six super skills, the tools you will need to turn your dreams into reality. Think of your favorite video game. You have to learn skills to advance to mastery of the game. Just as you get to try on roles in video games, each of these super skills allows you to imagine yourself with a new superpower. The more tools you unlock, the better you get at fighting off the opponents or being the last man standing in *Fortnite*. The benefit of each super skill is listed in terms of the executive functioning components it builds.

1. *Finding gifts* will increase emotion regulation, flexible thinking, and planning.

2. *Setting goals* will increase planning and emotion regulation, and help manage impulsiveness.

3. *Chunking* (breaking big goals down into small, manageable chunks) will increase attention, planning, and flexible thinking.

4. *Boosting motivation* will increase flexible thinking, impulse control, and emotion regulation.

5. *Managing mood* will increase emotion regulation, attention, and planning.

6. *Finding focus* will increase attention, planning, and impulse control.

These tools can be logically sequenced, and this is the sequence the book will follow. Finding gifts precedes setting goals because you want to focus on your innate talents, interests, and past successes to make sure that self-doubt doesn't lead you to set your goals too small. Chunking allows you to break goals into small elements that feel easily manageable. When you get to that point where you just don't feel like taking the next step, boosting motivation will get you through the fog of resistance. Managing mood will prevent you from getting derailed by impulses and other emotional upsets. And finally, finding focus will allow you to stay focused for longer periods of time, like increasing the battery life of your flashlight.

When you wonder how you will get from your goal to making your dream come true, try to think of it not as a chore but rather as a tournament testing your wits. You can use these tools in sequence to solve specific problems or combine them in response to the demands of a specific goal.

The most pressing and common goal for many teens is related to schoolwork. Because most teens struggle with the question of how to prioritize schoolwork, let's start with how one teen, Daniel, used two super skills—setting goals and chunking—to tackle that problem with a weekly strategy.

On Monday, Daniel created a list of what he has to do and by when:

What	By When
Study for math quiz	Quiz on Wednesday
Read and annotate online article for extra credit in government (optional)	Due Friday
Study for bio test	Test on Thursday
Write outline for English paper	Due Tuesday
Read 1 chapter of book for English for class discussion	Due Wednesday
History worksheet	Due Tuesday
Math problems	Due Wednesday

That's a lot of things to think about doing at once. Should Daniel go ahead and do them in order of their due dates? He could, but then he might not be using his time well. He has extra time on Tuesday but no time on Wednesday, so Tuesday is when he should study for his biology test and Wednesday is when he can do the optional extra credit assignment for government. Or maybe because he's doing fantastically in government he doesn't need to even think about the extra credit assignment.

Speaking of testing your wits, if you would like to try this out for yourself, go ahead and look at your schoolwork for the next week in terms of due dates and the time available for you to do each assignment. To help you prioritize school-related tasks, ask yourself these questions:

- *What is my current grade in each class?*

- *Which classes need more/less attention because I am not or am doing well?*

- *What are the due dates for each task?*

- *How much studying do I need to do based upon the material being tested?*

- *What will take the most time? The least time?*

- *Is there anything I will need extra help on?*

- *If yes, who can provide that help (for example, a friend, a teacher)?*

TRY IT Using your journal or Notes app, write down the dates of all your tests. and due dates for assignments for the next week of school. Then create a schedule of dates for you to complete your work.

By combining goal setting and chunking to create a strategy to finish homework and study for tests, you can prioritize what needs to happen and when. This will in turn increase your attention because you won't be stressing about when you need to do what, and you will be focused in on the task at hand.

If you're an ambitious teen determined to improve your executive functioning, there is truly nothing better than crossing a "to do" off the list, and nothing better than finishing that last "to do"! This is an example of how the goal setting and chunking super skills can be combined to help you work toward specific goals.

Why You Need to Beef Up Your Executive Functioning

Building your executive functioning by using the six super skills in this book is preventive medicine. For example, it is common to feel anxiety before a big test or a big game. The problem is that anxiety interferes with attention—one of the big five components of executive functioning. Anxiety can become a vicious cycle. The more anxious you are, the less you can concentrate, and then you really start to spaz out. If you can use some of the mood-managing tools to manage your anxiety, you can stay calm and confident. A simple example of taking charge of overwhelming emotions is to breathe out deeply a few times and say positive messages to yourself, such as *You can do this. Stay focused.*

As you're reading, you might start to stress out trying to figure out the six super skills and the five core components of executive functioning and how they all relate to each other. This would be a good chance to try out some encouraging self-talk.

Positive Self-Talk

Tell yourself, *I don't have to memorize any of this for a test! I'll just relax and focus on helpful tips that I can take action on.*

Or: *The more I read, the more it will make sense. These things take time. I can always reread, skim, or review selected parts as needed.*

Using Self-Talk to Manage Stress and Stop Bad Habits

The super skills are like medicine, and self-talk is the delivery method that creates lasting change rather than a small dose of inspirational feeling. Self-talk challenges negative thinking by replacing it with conscious, more positive thoughts. Think of it as being a coach or cheerleader to yourself.

Managing stress will help you access the super skills. If your brain is hijacked by stress, you may forget to use these skills. You may want to create an index card with a list of the six super skills so that if you feel overwhelmed in the moment, you can choose a skill to chart a new course, rather than getting more and more anxious and feeling like the world is closing in on you. You can say a positive statement silently or out loud. You can create a reminder for yourself by writing down your self-talk statement and putting it in a place where you will see it easily.

Many teens use nicotine, alcohol, and other drugs in an effort to feel better, concentrate more, and manage their moods (in other words, to manage a few of the main components of executive functioning). If you're using any of these substances to cope with stress, you can stop these bad habits by using the tools in this book to manage your stress. You can begin to see that using substances to control your brain is really a lack of finding other solutions to get the results you want. For example, if you need to calm down to focus, nicotine or weed should not be your first choice due to the risk they pose for your health and the potential for addiction. Tools like breathing exercises, positive self-talk, and mindfulness meditation (which we will get to in chapter 7) all have calming and focusing effects, and no downside. This book will give you lots of possible ways to feel better and stay focused.

Positive Self-Talk

Tell yourself, *Using drugs and alcohol to manage my mood is a treacherous path to take. I'll use super skills instead!*

Dr. Lara Says

A simple way to avoid nicotine and weed is to ask yourself, **How can I feel better or focus more?** *You can even create a list for yourself, such as taking a break, taking a few deep breaths, doing some stretches, getting some exercise, or listening to music.*

Some teens use video games or social media to numb their real-world anxieties. These habits can take up so much time that they prevent you from doing what needs to be done to solve real- world problems. If you typically spend two hours a day on video games, think how much more prepared you could be for those nerve-wracking tests if you used those hours to study calmly rather than at the last minute. Or think about your health and fitness goals. Think how many healthy choices you could make in those two hours you are spending on video games, streaming TV shows, or social media.

Getting Real About the Costs of Distractions

Think how much better your grades could be if you cut out one hour of mindless distraction, be it social media or watching your favorite YouTuber, and used that extra hour to prepare, plan, and study for your hardest class. You could take the biggest stressor in your life and feel like a champ by achieving mastery in one extra hour a day.

Research has shown that on average teens spend seven hours and twenty-two minutes a day on screens using media that doesn't involve schoolwork (Rideout and Robb 2019). These activities include social media, video games, watching online videos, watching TV, browsing websites, and listening to music.

If you are doing much better than that, think of everything else you can achieve in just three hours a day:

- You could train in a new skill, such as playing an instrument.

- You could take a class that would open up new opportunities, such as computer coding.

- You could get a job and start saving money to support some of your long-term goals or save for college.

- You could get more involved in organizations you belong to, whether it be a religious institution, special-interest group, or volunteer organization.

- You could spend time in meal preparation and exercising to help you achieve your health and fitness goals.

- You could take breaks and do more self-care! Activities like rest, napping, meditation, listening to music, and spending time in nature are highly restorative.

You can start small and see major progress by turning one hour of distraction into one hour of goal-directed activity. You don't have to take major risks. You can make shifts in low-stakes areas and see the freedom that comes in these more controlled experiments.

When you are streaming the first episode of *Gilmore Girls* on Netflix it might be easy to think, *I had a hard day at school, and I deserve a break.* However, by the time you are binge-watching your third episode, it gets hard to find any realistic benefits.

Positive Self-Talk

Ask yourself, *What are the benefits of this distraction?*

What Is Executive Dysfunction Anyway?

Some big terms used in talking about executive functioning include "impulse inhibition," "decision making," and "self-monitoring." Your executive functioning is like a parent nagging you to stop playing video games, get your homework done, and notice when you are talking too loud or being mean to your sister.

Executive functioning involves the prefrontal cortex, the brain structure that is close to your forehead. Because the human brain does not fully develop until the age of twenty-five, executive function skills can be even harder for teens; they may struggle more with the steps of setting a goal, breaking it down into steps, taking action, staying focused, and getting organized.

Before we delve much further into boosting executive functioning, you might want to know a bit more about *executive dysfunction*. Executive dysfunction is an impairment in thought, emotion regulation, or behavior that makes it difficult to get from goal setting to goal getting. Executive dysfunction is like a fever—it is a sign that something is wrong but doesn't give us any information about what is causing the dysfunction. When you have a fever, it is important to determine its cause. Is it a virus, a bacterial infection, inflammation, or something more serious? Similarly, there are many possible causes of executive dysfunction: ADHD, autism, sensory processing disorders, mood disorders, and traumatic brain injuries, among others.

Not all teens will have an executive dysfunction. Whether you have a diagnosis or not, any of these behaviors can be improved using the skills taught in this book:

- disorganization

- interrupting others

- anger outbursts

- being late getting assignments in

- not following directions

- being late for class and other events

You don't have to have a dysfunction to benefit from this book. All of us have some of these problems from time to time.

This book is not meant only for teens with executive dysfunction; it also will help anyone who wants to find productivity hacks or brain hacks. Every teen needs to set goals to get where they want to go, so this isn't about patching up weaknesses. Every teen has a prefrontal cortex that is still developing until around the age of twenty-five. This book will help you take a growth mind-set toward your attention, planning, flexible thinking, emotion regulation, and impulse control.

CHAPTER 2

Finding Gifts

The purpose of life is to discover your gift.
The work of life is to develop it.
The meaning of life is to give your gift away.

—David S. Viscott

You want to build your confidence before you set your goals so you feel capable of stepping outside your comfort zone. Finding positives will increase your determination—that means the chance that you will keep going when the going gets tough. Confidence will also increase your motivation, which affects the likelihood that you will actually just get started. Research has shown that if teachers were told that students were super-stars, those students—even though they were not actually higher in intelligence—improved their IQ at the end of the year. This has been called the self-fulfilling prophecy effect. A positive self-concept will allow you to develop your talents and interests. By finding your strengths, interests, and talents, you can develop notable mastery of something, rather than think-ing only in terms of patching up your weaknesses.

Your gifts can include:

- interests such as sports or helping children

- talents such as being good at math or creative writing

- personality leanings such as extraversion or introversion

- values such as hard work or helping others

Finding Your Own Strengths

To be your own strength finder, you can get started by writing down ten of your biggest past successes in your journal or smartphone Notes app. Your list might include a good grade on a test, making a new friend at camp, or scoring a goal in a championship game, among many other possibilities.

As you read through the list, what can you figure out about your gifts? Are you a good problem solver? Do you make friends easily? Are you creative? Are you a strong leader? Are you great at math and science?

Here are three different ways to go about figuring out your strengths:

- Write down three adjectives that summarize your pattern of success.

- Choose five people you trust and ask them to tell you what they see as your three biggest strengths. Think of yourself as doing research.

- In your journal or Notes app, write down five interests you have.

Abilities take practice and time to develop, so you may find you have interests in arenas where you don't have obvious abilities. If that's true for you, consider taking lessons or classes. For example, you may love to look at art but haven't taken any courses or practice in drawing or painting. You can test out that interest by searching out tutorials on YouTube.

The more you focus on your past successes and seek feedback on your strengths, the more you are likely to believe that if you try something, you have what it takes to succeed. You will be willing to work harder and adopt a growth mind-set—the idea that the harder you try, the more likely you are to succeed. For example, thinking, *I am disorganized* reflects a fixed mind-set and makes it harder for you to improve in that area. If instead you think, *The harder I try, the more organized I will be*—a growth mind-set—you are likely to make improvements in this area.

Your ability to achieve your goals will likely depend primarily on persistence. How hard are you willing to work? When you get frustrated that something is too hard or is taking too long, will you keep going?

That's why we focus on finding gifts and building confidence—because that will keep you going when you are faced with challenges.

Creating an Emergency Rescue Kit for Self-Doubt

Self-doubt is a lack of confidence that you can succeed at goals you have for yourself. It creates hesitation, a tendency to make excuses, and a failure to assert yourself in the service of achieving your goals. Shakespeare probably expressed it best in his play *Measure for Measure* when he said, "Our doubts are traitors, and make us lose the good we oft might win by fearing to attempt." Artist Vincent Van Gogh offered us one of the best solutions to self-doubt: "If you hear a voice within you say 'You cannot paint,' then by all means paint, and that voice will be silenced."

Self-doubt is often caused by specific failures we have had. The irony is that it is a distorted thought to think that failure is … actually a failure. If people were self-aware, they would talk about failure as itself a stepping-stone to success. People talk about their successes but they don't talk about their failures, so we mistakenly think that failure is final.

• *Susan's Story*

Susan had ADHD, and she didn't have a lot of success in high school. She did poorly on the SAT and was filled with self-doubt. She went to a community college, where she reached out for support, and with fewer classes and more time than she had had in high school, she got good grades. She took an SAT preparation class and began using Khan Academy's free SAT practice program to boost her scores. She raised her score by 200 points and was able to transfer to a state university. At the university, she realized that she wanted to be a therapist working with children. She applied to a graduate program in counseling and was accepted.

Some people with ADHD find success in school when they find an area of study they are enthusiastic about. Failure in high school was not final for Susan. She went on to a career in counseling children, and she was able to encourage them with her own story about struggles in school.

Notice when you feel self-doubt, and label it "self-doubt." Think of what you would say to a best friend who was doubting themselves. Say it to yourself. Create an "emergency rescue kit" for yourself—and use it!

TRY IT Research has shown that being happy increases success and productivity. Write a list of your past successes and a list of your five happiest memories. Keep this emergency rescue kit on your Notes app on your phone or take a photo of your list in a journal and keep it on your phone. You can create a folder called "Super Skills."

Remember that every point of failure can be the beginning of a hero's journey. Think of the story line of many movies: a person goes after a big dream and has a major defeat. What happens next? It wouldn't be a satisfying movie if the hero decided they were unlucky or untalented and just went back to life before the big goal. Here are some other ways you can handle defeat:

- You can practice having compassion for yourself as you would for a friend who had a failure experience.

- You can ask yourself, *Who can help me?*

- You can ask yourself, *What are some possible solutions?*

- You can ask yourself, *What kind of courses do I need to take to get better?*

- You can read an inspirational book to increase motivation and determination. Consider using this book as a mind builder's guide to your brain.

Reviewing your emergency rescue kit will help you restore a sense of self-efficacy—the belief that you are capable of accomplishing your goals and solving problems that arise as you move forward. A guiding sense of your strengths and capabilities will put your problems in perspective and give you a sense of control for managing your emotions.

Finding gifts will help you feel good, which will help you focus. It's important to remember that as you build each super skill you are positively impacting other super skills too—in this case, attention management.

Owning Your Interest and Talents

It's important to own your interests and talents because of the tendency to compare ourselves to others. If you know someone who is a great athlete, you may feel you are lacking something unless you can remind yourself of everything you are talented at. You can think of talents as the different types of classes, such as math, literature, science, and languages. You can also think of categories, such as artistic, musical, athletic, entertaining, academic, technology wiz, and more.

TRY IT   Write down five of your interests and talents in your journal or Notes app. You can label the folder in the notes section "Super Skills." What are five reasons you can be successful at each?

Job Description: Teenager

If being a teenager were a job, it would require certain mind-sets. The explorer, elite competitor, evolver, and investigator are different archetypes you can use to discover your strengths to set goals. You will want to try out each of these mind-sets; each might lead to finding a different strength. An explorer will find new interests, an elite competitor will find new talents, an evolver can develop new personality traits, and an investigator will find what they value.

You may have realized from the previous exercise that you need to explore the world more to find more interests. Additionally, you can't really know if something is really a talent unless you actually test yourself through hard work—wanting to be an elite competitor. You have to want to evolve to stretch out your personality traits. And finally, how are you going to find what you value if you are not willing to investigate?

You're not supposed to have it figured out. Finding your interests, talents, personality traits, and values is a journey you are just setting out on! Discovering these are part of your job description as a teenager.

Wanted: Explorer

To be an explorer is to discover new roles, new classes, new interests, new aspects of yourself. To explore means to try things outside your comfort zone. An adventure means going into the unknown, such as going to explore a meditation group or a worship service even if your family isn't religious. It could mean going on a trip with your friend's family and seeing what other families are like. It could mean taking a guitar class in high school even though you've never played an instrument. It could also mean reaching out to people who are in a different social circle than you. It could mean joining the robotics club even though you're more the literary type. Being an explorer could mean accepting invitations you might otherwise turn down.

Wanted: Elite Competitor

Take your game to a new level—you may have to upgrade to thrive. You don't really know what your skills, talents, and abilities are until you put the pedal to the metal, or really give it your all.

When you upgrade in life, just as when you upgrade your phone's operating system, it takes time to adjust to all the changes. If you decide to try something new, remember that every new skill, talent, and ability comes with a learning curve. In the beginning, you will put in a lot of effort to get little results. There may come a point of maximum frustration where you think, *I'm working so hard, but I'm just not good at it.* Don't quit at that point! On the learning curve, you will eventually turn the corner and feel some level of skill, and the more you practice, the more capable you will feel. Every time you devote yourself to learning a new skill or ability, remind yourself there is a necessary learning curve before thinking this is not your cup of tea.

Wanted: Evolver

Evolve into a more resilient, resourceful, stronger person. Being a teenager is challenging. Your executive functioning will not finish developing until you reach the age of twenty-five, and yet the demands on you are immense. One way to protect yourself from getting depressed about the many pressures is to think of each challenge as an opportunity to build strength in focusing, planning, and emotional resilience. The tools in this book will show you how to meet these challenges.

Every time you predict an obstacle and create a plan B, you are building the path to being unstoppable. Each time you feel overwhelmed that you have two tests to study for and you decide to break your evening up into fifteen-minute study periods with breaks in between and rewards at the end of each hour, you are learning how to increase motivation and sustain attention. To evolve means to expand your outlook beyond your comfort zone.

Wanted: Investigator

Investigation is the process of getting curious and being willing to test things out to see what really fits for you and find your values. For example, if you realize that you value learning new things, you can develop hobbies that have nothing to do with getting good grades. Learning becomes a value in itself, not just a means to an end. You may join an astronomy club not because you want to be an astronomer but because you love learning about space. In addition, your love of learning becomes a powerful tool for regulating your emotions. It may be that your interest in looking at the stars at night gives you such a sense of awe that it puts your personal challenges in perspective. The idea here is to try out new things to gain self-knowledge about your own values.

Now that you have some mind-sets for expanding and finding your interests, talents, and gifts, where do you want to go?

There Are Benefits to Unfocus

You might be happy to learn that science shows us there is a gift in unfocus. Research is finding that the part of the brain that is devoted to unfocus—the default mode network—is the source for many talents and abilities, including creativity. And as important as it is to develop executive functioning, creativity is also important. As you focus on strengths, don't rule it out! In my books *The Gift of ADHD* (Honos-Webb 2008) and *The ADHD Workbook for Teens* (Honos-Webb 2011), I describe five gifts of ADHD—creativity, empathy, emotional sensitivity, exuberance, and being nature smart. Which of these gifts do you think you have?

Recent research has shown that ADHD students are better than non-ADHD students at divergent thinking and creating new inventions (White 2019). The state of unfocus may be required to think outside the box. The phrases "sit on it" and "sleep on it" reflect this deep understanding that we have to give our brain a rest to make a breakthrough. In fact, the word "incubation" part of our common language as being essential for creativity. It requires us to turn attention away from a problem we are trying to solve in order to solve it. The primary definition of incubation includes an animal sitting on an egg waiting for it to hatch. So too with an idea—something new and creative will hatch if we "sit on it."

One way of understanding the relationship between unfocus and incubation and inspiration is through the legendary stories of inventor Thomas Edison, who some argue is a model of the distractible brain (Hartmann 2015). The prevailing image of Edison is that he worked on dozens of projects at the same time, focusing on one project until he got bored, then switching to another, and then to another. To switch from one project to another is consistent with the idea of incubation as a stage of creativity. Like the duck that sits on an egg waiting for it to hatch, so our creative inspiration requires this unfocused patience until the eureka moment when an answer seemingly magically presents itself.

So as you define your strengths and begin to build your executive functioning, don't rule out the importance of nurturing your creativity and giving yourself time to be unfocused.

In the Flow

Your natural talents and interests are usually activities that activate a sense of flow. Flow, being "in the zone" or fully engaged in an activity, makes time pass by like it is nothing, as if you aren't "working" at all. Because your mind is fully devoted to a certain activity and is using nearly all its concentration powers, it does not worry about things that are not pertinent to that activity (for example, time, birds chirping outside, a radio playing in the background). Rather than giving your attention to distractions, you become fully invested in the task or tasks at hand.

We pay more attention to what is interesting to us. Notice where you are in flow, and you will likely be finding a natural gift of yours. As you go through your week, notice which activities, classes, or events create this sense of being able to pay attention easily without effort. For the sake of this challenge, exclude video games and social media. Our goal here is to help you find healthy pleasures, possible career directions, areas of study, and talents to develop.

Competition: Its Benefits and Costs

Once you figure out what gets you in flow, you still have another obstacle to confront: competition. High school can make it complicated to find what your true interests are. It's easy to see what other people think is most important and to be influenced by that.

Maybe the highlight of your week is band practice, but other kids don't think it's cool. You don't want to leave your teen years realizing that almost every choice you made was driven not by who you really are, what you are really good at, and what you really wanted, but instead by what everybody else thought was cool or important. It doesn't matter whether someone else is better than you in sports if you're not interested in sports. You can overcome competitiveness by valuing the talents you do have.

Benefits of Competition

One benefit of competition is that it can be a huge motivator. If competition is a driving force for you, you want to have a sense of balance. Some people appear to have competitiveness as a personality trait, and it would be unwise to devalue that natural aspect of their personality. A competitive spirit can foster team spirit, but it also can lead to injuries if being the best comes at all costs. While competition can boost motivation, compare those benefits with the powerhouse boost that comes from working in your flow state, at something that comes easily to you. In fact, one might say that competition itself is not bad if you are already working in your area of strength.

Costs of Competition

Competition with others can be a trap. It's too easy to try to compete with others rather than doing the work of figuring out what you really value yourself. Competition can provide enormous drive, but it can derail you from what you really love. Competition can keep you narrowly focused on doing better than someone else rather than developing your talents and investing in yourself and your unique profile of gifts. It's possible to get addicted to competition and focus on being better than others instead of discovering who you are. Competition can lead you to feel dissatisfied even when you are excelling. There will always be people ahead of you and people behind you.

The drive to be better can create a lot of stress, which can interfere with optimal performance. Competition can become toxic when it takes you away from figuring out your own areas of real interest and flow.

Finding Those Who "Get" You

Finding validation for your gifts may mean focusing on the people who are paying close enough attention to "get" you. You may need only one or two people who really appreciate your unique talents, but the more people you can find to support you, the more you will value your own interests and talents.

As you start to focus on developing your gifts, keep your eyes trained on those who support you, and put blinders on those who are unthinkingly negative. Like a teen who focuses only on their friends' smiling faces in a crowd at a talent show, you too can block out discouraging and distracting voices. Even if you are really good at something, some people will feel jealous and challenge you even more. I wish I could tell you this happens only in high school, but many people, fueled by their own self-doubt, find it difficult to encourage others.

One of the best ways to find people who get you is to reach out to new people. Make it a goal to talk to one new person at school every day. Set a goal to talk to someone who is in a different crowd than you are. If you play a sport, ask a team member you haven't spent time with to go out for a smoothie after practice. You can never predict where you will find the person who gets you.

Overcoming Bad Feelings from Past Failures

Finding your strengths means getting over previous failures. It's all too common for teens and even adults to let previous failures prevent them from moving forward. Being failure phobic can lead to avoiding risk, which is necessary for success. The best way to get over any fear is by exposing yourself to it; the more you do something you are afraid of, the easier it gets to do. Fear of failure impairs many people, keeping them stuck in small lives because they are afraid of breaking their constant state of approving nods from their environment. When you lose your fear of failure, you gain the power to experiment in life and work, to try things outside your comfort zone and expertise. Experimentation leads to innovation and discovery, and you can become unstoppable. As you try out new skills and test your strengths, don't be afraid to fail.

After a failure, you will need to choose positive thinking and to challenge negative thinking. Negative thinking involves negative thoughts that hold us back from success. This can mean thinking you failed because of who you are rather than thinking you need a different strategy. Positive thinking means defining yourself by your gifts and talents rather than setbacks and weaknesses.

If you think of yourself as one of a kind, you can open to the idea that your talents may be different from others'. It may be that you find only a few people who really get you and recognize your talents. Pay attention to those people! Give yourself permission to experiment with goals, learn about yourself, and feed that learning back into new goals.

CHAPTER 3

Setting Goals

People who set goals are more likely to succeed than people who do not. Having explicit objectives that are challenging and specific—with clear timeline[s] and performance criteria—leads to better performance.

—Tal Ben-Shahar

Now that you have found your gifts, you will be choosing your goals. Goal setting starts with taking the time to think of all the accomplishments you want to achieve in your own life. This chapter guides you through setting goals that are meaningful to you and are a bit of a stretch so you gain a sense of mastery. The combination of autonomy, purpose, and mastery are fuel to create motivation and drive (Pink 2009).

Many people think of goal setting as something you do once a year, perhaps on New Year's Eve or at the beginning of the school year. The new year starts off as a seemingly fresh slate, inviting us to decide that this year will be different. This once-a-year excitement is a bit silly, because planning is a fundamental component of our executive functioning; we should be using it every day—in fact, every hour!

If you have ADHD, planning can be a particular challenge. For example, people with ADHD:

- struggle with time management

- struggle with overcoming resistance to take action on future goals

- are more impulsive

- may not pay attention to consequences that will occur in the distant future

Those who struggle with executive dysfunction may think only as far as the next hour or day, whereas others can plan for a week, month, or year ahead. This is why goal setting is so helpful—it is setting time aside to plan.

Let's start with a common goal many teenagers have—getting good grades. Once you set the goal, it gives you a sense of purpose that narrows your focus. The more focused you are, the more clarity you will have in understanding material and your communications with other people. Once you decide to get good grades, the decision shifts your priorities and helps you figure out what is a distraction and what is not. For example, if you want to get a good grade on your Spanish test, what becomes a higher priority—finishing season five of your favorite show or finding a partner to practice your Spanish with before the test?

With a targeted goal, your priorities suddenly become clear. Goal setting will help you figure out what to prioritize and what to say no to. You might find that spending time on mindless streaming of entertainment, social media, and video games will have to take a back seat. As you think about getting a good grade on your Spanish test, you might start by writing a list of friends who may be able to study with you. Next, you could look at your schedule and create a list of best times to connect with a friend, and then you can text friends with times you have available and determine who has a match.

Benefits of Goal Setting

A goal directs activity, increases motivation, and gives you a purpose—all of which help you focus more throughout the day. That focus will empower you to solve problems and make clear decisions. A goal motivates you, because once you set it, a certain need to prove to yourself that you can do it kicks in.

Think of a goal in the literal sense on a hockey rink, or football or soccer field. What if you played those sports, but there was no scoring, and therefore no winner or loser? That could be fun and a good way to get exercise, but how focused would you be with no actual goal? If you didn't care about scoring goals, would you ever come up with a playbook or a strategy? Probably not. The goal drives you to practice your drills of passing and scoring.

When we have goals, we usually have to upgrade all areas of our lives in order to achieve them. Even if we don't get a specific goal or win a game, we are most likely going to develop new skills in the pursuit of the goal. The bottom line is this: when you have a goal, you try harder.

Trying harder will include taking the time to organize yourself before you start working. When you sit down to do your homework, you may have many papers in your backpack, half-read books that need to be completed, folders, and a calendar. If your goal is to get good grades, you will try harder to plan your strategy for that evening. While doing your homework in the moment may not feel good, if you see it as a stepping-stone to your goal of good grades, your motivation will be enhanced.

Goals also boost your mood. One researcher found that the process of striving for goals is an essential component of happiness (Ben-Shahar 2007). Achieving a goal also increases your sense of self-efficacy—your feeling of confidence to achieve specific tasks (Locke and Latham 2002).

A goal allows you to feel optimistic that the future can be different from where you are now. If you set a small goal and attain it, you get a sense of satisfaction. If you set a daily goal to limit social media, you may feel a sense of accomplishment every time you resist picking up your phone to check Snapchat.

Attaining longer-term goals can change your self-image. If you successfully achieve a goal of getting an A in a class that previously felt out of reach, you can begin to think more broadly of your own capacity to succeed. Setting goals can help you manage anxiety by giving you a sense of control over a situation. Rather than fearing you will get a bad grade, you realize you can affect the outcome. Your grade on your next test doesn't depend on how smart you are but on how hard you work.

Goals allow you to act more intentionally and promote a growth mind-set (Dweck 2007). This is in contrast to the fixed mind-set—here, the belief that some people are smart and others are not as smart. The growth mind-set will transform your fear of failure into a commitment to work harder and challenge yourself.

Former president John F. Kennedy's speech launching the United States into the space race offers an example of how we ourselves are transformed by goals: "We choose to go to the moon in this decade and do the other things, not because they are easy, but because they are hard, because that goal will serve to organize and measure the best of our energies and skills, because that challenge is one that we are willing to accept, one we are unwilling to postpone, and one which we intend to win, and the others, too." This goal is a great example of something that seemed almost impossible at the time, yet has led to a long history of space travel, and many private space industry companies such as SpaceX and Blue Origin that are taking us into a future that is starting to look like a lot of science fiction.

Goals are great tools for managing the impulsive behavior that comes with ADHD and other executive functioning difficulties. Goals essentially redirect your attention away from the resistance you feel in the moment and toward a positive outcome. For example, you can set a goal to reduce your smartphone use. Setting this goal will keep you from being distracted and serve as a reminder to stay on track. When you think of your goal, it may help you pause and delay picking up that phone that can turn into a brain drain. Goals can be aids to mindfulness. They set a momentary barrier between impulse and action, allowing us to act more intentionally.

Francine shares her story of overcoming the obstacle of doing something that feels too hard.

• *Francine's Story: Pushing Back Against the Impossible*

Sometimes it's hard to set a goal because you don't really feel it's possible. I have a friend who traveled to Europe several times a year to visit family. She invited me to visit her in Europe for sightseeing and adventure. I always said, "yeah sure, someday," but mostly I said that to get her off my back. For me, to take a trip to Europe seemed impossible. I was worried about money, and I was afraid of flying and what could go wrong with so many unknowns.

One day she said to me, "I think the problem is you really think it's impossible." I didn't hesitate to say that was exactly what it seemed to me. There were so many stressors in my life of competing needs that planning and paying for a trip to Europe did seem impossible. She told me, "It's not impossible. It's just one plane flight and next thing you know you're in Europe; it's really not a big deal." I wasn't convinced but I did set a goal to go to Europe. I realized that if I saved money over the summer it would seem sort of manageable.

With the goal in mind, I worked some odd jobs scooping ice cream and some retail sales. As I approached graduation, some friends were planning a trip to Europe, and I said I wanted to make it happen. With a little planning, I was able to buy a plane ticket to London to visit my friend.

Dr. Lara Says

One lesson from Francine's story is straightforward: If there's something you want to accomplish but it seems impossible, find someone who already does that. Talk to them and learn how to break it down into manageable steps.

SMART Goals

Before we get deeper into goal setting, let's talk about SMART goals. When you create your goals, you want to make sure they are concrete enough for you to achieve them and know when you have achieved them.

Below is a formula and an example for creating goals that will motivate you and increase your chances of success.

S—Specific

When Michael was going to a new high school where most of the kids would know everybody, he said he wanted to make new friends. I helped him set up two specific goals: (1) I will talk to one person in each class the first week I start school and (2) I will join clubs as a way to meet people who share interests with me.

M—Measurable

Michael decided to create a checklist of all his classes for the first week of school. Each time he gathered the courage to talk to someone in a class, he could check off that class. He decided he would test out three different clubs: the Homework Club, the Chess Club, and the Gay-Straight Alliance Club. After trying out all three clubs, he would choose one to commit to.

A—Attainable

Talking to one person in every class was attainable; Michael had control over it and the courage to take a risk. His goal was to join a chess club, not to win a national chess title. He doesn't have control over the team's performance. His motivation was to find friends with shared interests, and he did not have the skill level to win a national title.

R—Relevant

Making new friends is relevant because Michael's level of satisfaction at his new high school will be increased by feeling socially connected. A sense of belonging is one of the most important needs of any teenager.

T—Time Bound

Michael chose the time frame of talking to people in the first week of class because he realized that he would have his best chance of meeting other new people before cliques started to form, and he would gain confidence by starting out strong.

In summary, SMART goals allow you to monitor your progress toward your goal, to know if you are on track. You can check off elements, such as introducing yourself to a new person. SMART goals also help you figure out what you have control over and what you do not have control over. You can control how many people you reach out to. You cannot control if they like you, or even if they do, whether that will make you popular. You gain a sense of control over your life by clarifying what you can do and taking small steps in the right direction.

Writing Down Your Goals

Research has shown that writing down your goals will increase your chances of success. One study found that 70 percent of those who wrote down their goals reported progress in goal achievement, compared to 35 percent who didn't write down their goals (Matthews 2007). It may be that writing down a goal makes it go from a thought in your mind to a concrete reality you are now accountable for.

Every day we have wants, desires, and goals that go through our minds and are immediately followed by worries, concerns, and immediate demands in the real world. Our goals can be like fireworks, impressive but fading quickly from memory. In the constant stream of thoughts and feelings, our most important goals can easily get lost. Writing them down makes us take our goals seriously. It also forces us to think more clearly about the scale and scope of our goals.

Areas for Goal Setting

To get started setting goals, let's look at four important areas for goal setting: school, relationships, health and fitness, and bucket lists. We'll dig deeper into school goals because those tend to be the area of greatest importance and therefore stress for many teens.

School

It's necessary, as always with goals, to focus on the purpose. Ideally, your goals will have more to do with your values than with your ability. We often forget that the purpose of an education is not to chase grades—although striving to achieve the best grade possible will transition into other areas of your life—but to be educated, to learn. Some teens may aspire to getting all As or Bs; for others, the goal may be to avoid getting

Ds. You might pick subjects you are already interested in and focus on excelling in those classes.

Some examples of goals in an academic setting include:

- graduating

- achieving a certain grade on a specific test

- not missing any homework in a week (or month or quarter, or perhaps a year)

- studying x number of nights per week (or per month)

- scoring an A (or B or C) on a specific test (or paper or project)

In addition to grades, which is where the majority of goals will likely be set, are more intrinsic goals. We go to school for years in order to learn more about the outside world, but also to learn more about the inside world—ourselves. In order to figure out what you want to do, where you want to be, and who you want to be, you have to figure out what you don't want to do, where you don't want to be, and who you don't want to be.

TRY IT Take out your journal or the Notes app on your phone, and write down a mission statement for your education. Your mission statement should include your goal, the purpose of your goal, and one action step. For example:

- I want to get good grades and my ultimate purpose is to increase the opportunities I will have. I will create a study schedule and stick to it.

- I want to get a summer job at the Space and Science Center. The purpose is to prepare me to work in the private space industry. I will google the center and ask for more information.

- I want to work with animals. The purpose of my education is to prepare me to work in wildlife and environmental conservation. I will ask my family and teachers if they know someone who works in this field.

Remember to base your statement on a SMART goal—specific, measurable, attainable, relevant, and time bound. List one thing you will do in pursuit of the goal.

SEEK OUTSIDE SUPPORT

In working toward your school goals, you may need extra help. Many schools have resources for peer tutors, and many local libraries also offer peer tutoring services.

You could also consider seeing a school counselor or ther-apist. Some therapists are trained to help you manage atten-tion problems and address test-taking anxiety that can directly impact your grades. And just having someone to talk to can also help your grades because the things that bother you on a day-to-day basis can interfere with your attention and moti-vation. If, for example, your parents are getting a divorce or a family member is ill or struggling with an addiction, these can weigh heavily on you and distract you from your own goals. The phrase "just getting it off your chest" can be appli-cable—even if your problems don't magically go away, you will have more energy available for taking on your classwork. Talking with a therapist can help you learn tools for changing the channel to happy memories to replace worry, challenging self-defeating thoughts, and getting referrals to other support systems in your community.

Positive Self-Talk

Tell yourself, *I have to feel it to heal it. If I don't talk it out, I may act it out.*

SEEK ACCOMMODATIONS

If you have a diagnosis such as ADHD, autism, or a specific learning disorder, you may be able to receive specific accom-modations to help you with your schoolwork. These accommo-dations can include having a note taker in classes, getting to take tests in private rooms, or being allowed more time. Some students will be allowed to use speech-to-text technologies to do their schoolwork. There are also technologies, such as the C-PEN, that can be used to scan text and read it aloud to students who are wearing headphones.

Relationships

Although some teens value school goals more than relationship goals, research has consistently shown that happy people have one thing in common: they have strong social relationships. That is why super skill number one is finding gifts. You can build self-confidence that will help you make and keep friends.

First and foremost, in order to set relationship goals, you need to decide what you want. Do you want to have great friends and be a great friend? Do you want people to expand your world by showing you other families, other activities, other ways of understanding the world? Friends can make our world bigger and more interesting. Friends can support us and give us a broader perspective on life. Building connections with friends will help you in romantic relationships when you are ready for that. Having friends increases flexible thinking; when you realize they have different values, skills, and interests, the world can open up to you. You can also add great value to your friends' lives. You can inspire friends with your love of reading books or finding hidden gems of movies to watch.

TRY IT Think about the value you can add to a friend's life by being a friend as much as you benefit from having a friend. Using your journal or Notes app, write a list of five ways you can be a friend to someone else.

As you can start to see, there are a million reasons why people need social connections. For you, there may be just one, a few, or many. There can be a primary purpose, as well as secondary ones. You may change your purpose along the way to achieving that goal. No matter what happens, though, always keep in mind some sort of "why." Think of it like a rope that you're holding on to for dear life. If you let go of the "why" of your goal, your dream, it can lose meaning. You may still achieve it, but it likely won't mean anything to you anymore. And life is all about meaning.

TRY IT Write down three relationship goals in your journal or the Notes app on your phone—for example, to talk to one new person every week at school so you keep expanding your social circle; to find friends who share similar interests; or to find a caring dating relationship. Include the purpose of the goal, the ultimate "why?" Some people's social goals may be a means to an end—for example, they want to have friends so they have something to do on Saturday night. For other people, social goals are more abstract; they simply find being connected to others emotionally fulfilling in itself.

• *Dwayne's Story*

Dwayne wanted to be a nurse when he grew up, and he was frustrated that he didn't currently have anyone to share his interests or help him figure out how he could build his interest. He decided to join a club at high school for students interested in health careers. Through this club, he made friends with similar interests and learned about many exciting opportunities. He also took a class in administering CPR where he got to meet more people who were motivated to be helpers in the medical field. Through these social relationships, he gained vital information for directing his future. He found a local hospital that offered volunteer programs for high school students, and he set a goal to apply over the summer. He learned that when he was eighteen he could enroll in a certified nursing assistant program in his area. These actions and goals increased his motivation and gave him confidence for his long-term career goal. Equally important, this process built his social network and friendships. These friendships were easier because everyone's shared interests in health careers gave them so much to talk about.

Health and Fitness

Health and fitness goals can include, for example, having a healthy diet, setting up a regular exercise plan, or playing basketball in college. Setting a goal allows you to figure out whether you're on track, and if not, to find a strategy to get there.

Let's say you decide you want to run a marathon. Your primary purpose may be to prove to yourself that you can be disciplined. Your secondary purpose may be that you want to get healthier, be in better shape, eat better, or quit smoking. To help you decide the "why," ask yourself: Do I want to get in better shape? Is setting the goal of running a marathon a way to help me do that? Is it something to focus on to help me run? Do I just want to run more?

• *Olivia's Story*

Olivia set a goal to run a half marathon. Her purpose was to create a lifelong habit of running to stay fit and help her manage her emotions. She had noticed that when she got stressed out, she would spend time on Snapchat and Instagram, hoping they would distract her from her stress. Instead, she often found herself more stressed. Sometimes she saw a group of her friends hanging out without her. She felt ignored and rejected. She found that if she went for a run she would get a more balanced reaction to put social media in perspective.

Olivia thought running would have many healthy side effects and wouldn't create more angst for her, as social media did. She set daily running goals with scheduled breaks so she could recover or nurse injuries. She committed to running regularly and started out walking and running until she could run greater distances. She found friends to run with her. She monitored her thought process and disciplined herself to keep her thoughts encouraging. She found that remembering her purpose helped her keep motivated. She did achieve her goal and found that running helped her put in perspective the ups and downs of the daily social drama in high school.

One way to start tackling health and fitness is to set ninety-day goals. With a ninety-day goal, you will not have to wait too long to see progress or goal completion. Seeing that progress builds motivation to keep setting goals. The momentum you gain can help you avoid procrastination and build confidence.

Research has found that making a public commitment, such as sending your goal to a parent or friend, increases goal progress (Matthews 2007). Being accountable to others allows you to get support, encouragement, and helpful guidance from them. One way to do this is to send weekly progress reports to the people you made a public commitment to.

TRY IT   Write down three of your own health and fitness goals in your journal or Notes app, and include the purpose or bigger "why." Use the SMART goal formula to increase your level of success and ability to monitor your progress. Write down one actionable step you will take this week. Send an email to a friend or family member telling them about this step you will take.

Bucket List Goals

Even if your goals are not about what you're going to do with your life, the pursuit of bucket list goals can shape your answer to that question and clarify what you are capable of. Bucket list goals tend to involve travel, adventure, and experiences, rather than self-improvement.

In *100 Things: What's on Your List?*, author Sebastian Terry described the hundred items he wanted to accomplish, including running with the bulls and delivering a baby. While he fulfilled many of his goals, it was a simple one that transformed his life, giving him a vocation. That goal was to help a stranger. He helped a paralyzed man accomplish his dream of running a marathon by pushing him to the finish line. The sense of satisfaction he got from that experience led to his true dream of helping others by creating Kindsum.com, a platform where people could ask for help or give help. He began to travel around the world speaking. He was transformed by the goals he set to create his own happiness.

TRY IT Write down three of your bucket list goals in your journal or Notes app, and include the purpose or bigger "why." Use the SMART goal formula to increase your level of success and ability to monitor your progress. Write down one actionable step you will take this week.

• *Coretta's Story*

Coretta loved dogs but her parents wouldn't let her get one. Her bucket list goal was to spend a lot of time with dogs. Her first idea was to offer to walk the neighbors' dogs. She realized that she would have to sign up for a class on how to take care of dogs. She googled "teen classes to help dogs" and found a local Animal Rescue Foundation that offered classes, opportunities to be a teen counselor at summer camps, and lots of volunteer activities. She realized that she had more than enough opportunities to meet her bucket list goal. She made her ninety-day goal to complete a training on how to care for dogs and become an advocate for their welfare.

I hope this story inspires you to see that goals can transform not only your life but also your own confidence in yourself and your ability to stretch yourself. You have to step out of your everyday life to reach rewards that will test and increase your own skills and courage. Every time you step out of your comfort zone, which is required to achieve your goals, you get more and more able to expand that zone. Goals give you the sense that you are a creator of your life. Your life is not like a movie you have to sit down and watch unfold—you are the movie director, the screenwriter, and the actor.

CHAPTER 4

Chunking

Anyone can carry his burden, however heavy, until nightfall.
Anyone can do his work, however hard, for one day. Anyone
can live sweetly, patiently, lovingly, purely, until the sun
goes down. And this is all that life really means.

—Robert Louis Stevenson

Chunking—breaking big projects into smaller steps—can be the most powerful super skill for immediate results. It is also the simplest to learn and use instantly. Think of a messy desk you have to clean or laundry you have to do. You may feel resistance to it because it feels like a huge hassle. Now think of setting a timer for five minutes and telling yourself you will clean for five minutes and then stop even if you have not finished the job. Most people would be willing to get started because the project doesn't seem so big.

For many people, this simple tool creates change quickly. What if instead of piling up garbage in your car, you spent two minutes every day cleaning it out? The car would be clean, you wouldn't be embarrassed to drive your friends around, and you could find needed items quickly. Most people feel encouraged by their progress and gain momentum. One barrier to getting started can be the pressure to get it just right the first time. The desire to be perfect is in some ways the opposite of chunking. Psychologists often tell their clients that perfectionism can be self-defeating when it creates anxiety rather than progress.

• *Fernando's Story*

Fernando described himself as "an all-or-nothing guy." He didn't like the inbetween. When he worked out, he liked to go all out at the gym; if he couldn't do that, he wouldn't work out at all. When he made his lunch to take to school, he liked to imitate his favorite TV chef; if he couldn't do that, he would just bring money to buy lunch.

Because of his all-or-nothing style, he created a plan to work on his senior project only on weekends when he could spend from three to five hours at a time doing research, coming up with ideas, and devoting a significant amount of time to valuable work, all within one sitting.

The problem with that approach was that on the weekend he felt a great deal of resistance to getting started on spending such a long amount of time on focused work.

When I suggested to him that he spread out the work across the week in small chunks, he gave it a try. He still felt resistance and was tempted to tell himself that if he watched Netflix instead he could procrastinate until the weekend.

When he was able to get started, even if only for a half hour, and see some progress, he felt more accomplished and more satisfied.

In this case, Fernando was impacted by his own self-talk. He told himself that he could do a half hour on weekdays and it would all add up (helpful). But then he told himself that if he did it all on the weekend he could watch Netflix and get immediate gratification (unhelpful).

All of us have these helpful and unhelpful voices. There are some solutions that can get you to focus on the helpful, positive self-talk. For example, Fernando could say:

- *I can just write for ten minutes, and at least I will see some progress.*

- *I might enjoy Netflix more without the guilty feeling of the senior project hanging over my head.*

- *What's the smallest amount of time I am willing to put in now?* (This can help him recognize that maybe one hour is too long. He describes himself as "an all-or-nothing guy," so he may need to learn there are many options other than doing zero work during the week.)

- *Do I really want to let my resistance win again?* (This allows him to engage his determination to be the boss of his brain and not let his resistance win yet again.)

He could also think of someone who has a lot of strength, maybe the Rock (Dwayne Johnson). He could follow him on Instagram to seek inspiration for his ideal of being strong and to realize the benefits of hard work—in this case, lifting weights.

Decreasing Resistance Through Chunking

Think of each chunk as a stepping-stone on the path to your final destination. Stepping-stones decrease the level of resistance to getting started by making a job smaller. There are two different categories for chunking: routine and rhythm.

Routine Chunking

Routine can get boring, but it is steady, reliable, and simpler. People with inattentive ADHD may prefer routine because there is less distraction, making focus easier. With routine, you don't have to take up mental bandwidth to shift gears and figure out what's next. A routine is fixed, with prescribed amounts of time for work and prescribed amounts of time for breaks. If you think of stepping-stones, it would be equidistant stones in which all the stones were identical.

A simple example of routine chunking for doing your homework could include these stepping-stones:

- Finish your homework for one class.

- Take a break.

- Start homework for another class.

- Take a break.

- Repeat until you get to your reward, which is one hour of video games.

Some routine-oriented chunking methods have gained popularity; one example is the Pomodoro method. This strategy involves working for twenty-five minutes, then taking a break for five minutes. You would repeat four sets, then take a longer break. This strategy has the benefit of having a lot of accessories that go with it—an app, hourglasses you can flip over to measure the work and break time, and more.

Some people with executive function challenges need to find the right ratio of work to break time. It might be twenty minutes work to ten minutes break. Those with more severe challenges might even need fifteen minutes work to twenty minutes break. Although it is not the most efficient strategy, for some, it might be the only strategy that is motivating.

Rhythm Chunking

In contrast, rhythm chunking allows for responsive changes to meet your current needs and preferences. Times and breaks are not fixed. In the example of the stepping-stones, each stone can be different from the others; you could change your mind about how long you will work, how long you will rest, what kind of work you will do, and what rest time means.

While routine is fixed and stable, rhythm is changing, like the seasons of the year. Rhythm makes life interesting—in some parts of the country, just when the autumn leaves have finished falling, you get winter's first snow. Change is fun, but it is also work. You have to rake the leaves and then get out the snow shovel. It takes flexibility to adapt to the rhythm of life. People with impulsive/hyperactive ADHD may prefer rhythm because it is constantly changing and more stimulating.

Rhythm chunking could look like this:

- Have a snack.

- Study for an hour.

- Go for a fifteen-minute walk.

- Study for a half hour.

- Eat dinner.

- Study for a half hour.

- Check social media for fifteen minutes.

- Study for an hour.

- Watch Netflix for an hour before going to bed.

While this is not as strict as a routine-oriented Pomodoro-type study method, it far surpasses the free-for-all of coming home from school without a plan and watching TV, then procrastinating and opening up your books after dinner. For some teens with executive function challenges, just moving from this free-for-all to a rhythm-based structure can make a big difference.

When using rhythm chunking, you can recharge your brain by filling your breaks with activities that restore attention. Research has also shown that remembering happy times boosts mood and attention (Ben-Shahar 2007). The next activity allows you to access happy memories to boost attention.

TRY IT On your phone or laptop, create a photo folder labeled "Happy." Choose from twenty-five to fifty photos of your happiest memories, and put them in this folder. These may include photos of people you love, great times with friends, landmark sights you've been to, breathtaking scenery you've visited, or other things that make you smile or bring to mind some of the best times of your life. You can include happy memories that are selfies, but that shouldn't be the focus. The idea is to find times where you were emotionally connected or filled with positive feelings—not just flattering photos of yourself.

One of the other benefits of using a happy-photo file is that it can help you avoid the addictive trap of of social media. Not only can social media be addictive (in fact, it's designed to be so), but it can also create negative emotions, whether it be fear of missing out on what other people are doing or jealousy of what other people have. Boosting mood has been shown to increase productivity, so creating your own happy file gives you access to a customized attention-boosting tool.

TRY IT Using your journal or Notes app, write down your current after-school rhythm, including eating, home-work, exercise, and screen time. Review your list and see where you could add more productivity or tweak it so that you add more variety, like changes in the seasons. Do you need more color, more movement, more fun, or more mood brightening?

• *Moriah's Story*

Moriah had two big problems that kept her from getting the grades she wanted. One was social media, and the other was YouTube. She kept her phone near her while she did her homework and had alerts on from all her social media channels and texts from her friends and her swim team. She started to fix this by creating a routine of forty-five minutes studying followed by thirty-minute breaks. Her phone would be in another room during work times, so she was more efficient. She would allow herself to watch YouTube videos only during break times, and instead of becoming a distraction, it became a reward. She earned the reward only after she completed the forty-five-minute study period. After Moriah made these changes and got positive results, including improved grades, she realized she had been fooling herself by thinking that she could study and watch videos or track social media at the same time.

Advanced Chunking Strategies

Some people find that they don't want to even think about homework because the idea of opening their precalculus (or history or science) book is overwhelming. They don't start on anything because they are avoiding the mental quicksand they fall into thinking about their hardest subject. The point is that without creating a plan, your mind can turn homework into a monster lurking under the bed.

These advanced chunking strategies can help you handle the tasks you have the most resistance to.

Eating the Frog

The phrase "eat the frog" comes from the idea that if someone told you that you had to eat a frog you might waste a whole day thinking about how terrible that would be, rather than just getting it over with as soon as possible so you can enjoy the rest of your day (Tracy 2017). By doing your hardest homework first, you know that the rest of the homework will be easier. The relief of having the hardest thing done can be its own reward.

Deciding on Chunk Size

Break the hardest course into the smallest chunks. For example, if your worst class is Spanish, make a point of studying for a half hour on Saturdays and Sundays so you can do smaller chunks during the busier weekdays. You may have to create a rhythm that has more restoration time—activities that allow you to restore your brain—compared to your study time. It might be fifteen minutes study Spanish, twenty minutes listen to music. That's not efficient, but if that's what it takes to get going, it's worth a try.

Another way to facilitate chunking is to rate the level of resistance you have to certain tasks. The higher the resistance, the smaller the chunks you may need to feel motivated to get started. The level of resistance you feel may be a guide to creating a rhythm rather than a routine. For example, in planning an evening of study, you may want your first task to be a shortened time of study for your hardest class. The reward for overcoming the resistance may be a longer break time. If the resistance is overwhelming, ask yourself, *What is the smallest possible chunk I can do?* Most people will be able to dive in for ten minutes. If that's what you have to tell yourself to get started, give it a try.

Getting Started

Sometimes a task feels so overwhelming that you might not realize that some parts are harder than others, and that the first step is not the hardest. For example, if you have to study for a test, you may have to write out flash cards to study. You might realize that you don't mind writing out the flash cards— you can use colorful markers and have some fun with it—but it's the memorization that's hard. This question can help you get started and gain momentum. The process of making the flash cards adds variation to your study time, so there are benefits that exceed just borrowing someone else's flash cards. Even using pictures can help you by giving you more variation, which can be more stimulating.

Try to think of steps that move you forward and are more fun. For example, making flash cards may be more fun if you use markers with scents. You could read vocabulary words into your voice recorder on your phone and then listen to the recording before a big test to get in some review. You could have fun recording vocabulary words by using funny voices or singing them to the tune of your favorite song. Explaining the material you are learning to someone else is a great way to test out how well you have learned it.

SQR3

SQR3 is a study method that involves chunking studying into (S) scanning material; (Q) asking yourself questions; and

(R3) reading, reciting, and reviewing. Scanning means looking over chapter headings, skimming where you're interested, and getting a sense of what you will be covering. By asking questions, you prepare your mind to look for answers. You can think of any questions your teacher may have asked you to think about as you do the assignment. In addition to reading, reciting (or speaking out loud) as if you were teaching someone else can create a rhythm for studying. After doing all that, one final review can increase your retention.

It can be hard to start studying because you feel like you have to somehow get all the material from a chapter into your brain in one try. SQR3 offers you five different ways, some easier than others, to absorb the material.

One Thing at a Time

You can super boost the superpower of stepping-stones by following the slogan "One thing at a time." Many people think they're great at multitasking, but they are fooling themselves. Researchers have found that multitasking increases the amount of time it takes to get something done and also increases mistakes. Try to be honest with yourself. As much as you try to slog through your homework by having Netflix on in the background as a distraction, if you're honest, you'll notice it is exactly that—a distraction.

Chunking is an alternative to pointless distraction. You can use a TV show as a reward for completing a chunk that you feel motivated to do. It is likely you will get more done in fifteen minutes of focused work than in a longer time of distracted work. More important are the habits you are forming as you practice chunking. Switching tasks (homework and TV) creates anxiety and brain fog, and can become addictive because the novelty boosts your level of the brain chemical dopamine (Levitin 2015). Multitasking leads to lower quality work and over time depletes working memory.

"One thing at a time" offers a different quality of life. Your life is made up of a sequence of moments that pass by quickly, and when you are present in each moment, you enhance the quality of your life. You can choose to be fully present for your life or to go through life mindlessly.

• *Christopher's Story*

It was Monday, and Christopher had a paper on The Great Gatsby *due the next Monday. He had known about the assignment since the beginning of the semester and hadn't even bought the book yet. When he realized the paper was due in one week, he took the next step and downloaded the book on his Kindle. Every time he read for forty minutes, he would allow himself to play one game of* League of Legends.

As Christopher read, he would sometimes wonder what was going on. He would text his classmates who were also working on their papers and they talked about their respective ideas. They started a group text where they could ask questions, and they supported each other in trying to understand the themes of the book. Not only did he get new perspectives but also the support energized him to keep going. It turned out he wasn't the only one who had waited to the last week to start this assignment.

Christopher did finish his paper on Sunday evening, but he reflected on how stressful it was to spend his whole weekend doing a project that would have been a lot easier if he had started when he got the assignment, not one week before it was due.

Challenging Resistance

When I described goal setting in chapter 3, you learned that one of your greatest enemies can be called resistance. Quite simply, this is that feeling of "I don't feel like doing it now" or "I can do this later." Resistance is to be planned for and expected; you encounter it every single day. Chunking is one of your greatest allies in challenging resistance. The quickest way to challenge resistance is to figure out what the first step is. Then you set your goal as just that one simple step.

TRY IT Think about the project you have the most resistance to. Take out your journal or Notes app, and write down what the first step is. Make this step the smallest possible chunk.

Dr. Lara Says

One simple strategy for success in school is to start on an assignment when you get it. This strategy has the benefit of allowing you to work in smaller chunks. You can do a little over longer time so you will not have so much resistance to getting started. Stress interferes with attention, making it harder to focus. By working on a long-term project in small chunks over a lot of time, you won't feel so much stress and pressure. Starting early and working in small chunks is a win-win.

Whenever you don't feel like doing something, ask yourself, *What's the first step I can take?* or *What's the smallest step I can take right now?* Even if that first step is just writing out a list of what items you need to get started, you have already made your job a lot easier.

CHAPTER 5

Boosting Motivation

You cannot escape the responsibility of tomorrow by evading it today.

—Abraham Lincoln

Many people with ADHD and executive dysfunction believe that their lack of motivation is an unchanging quality of who they are. You may feel surprise and shock that there are things you can do to increase your motivation, and there are things you may be doing that decrease your motivation. One of the most common hurdles to motivation is a negative view of yourself, the idea that you are unmotivated because there's just something wrong with you. However, the good news is that motivation is a super skill, which means that it can be learned. In fact, thinking of motivation as a super skill can defeat these negative, internal, persistent beliefs about who you are and what you are capable of.

Think about it this way: if you were a baseball player, the more times you practiced hitting the ball, the better you would get at batting. So too with practicing the super skills: the more you practice, the better you will get. This may seem like common sense, but there's also a scientific explanation. One of the reasons you get better with practice is because of the brain's neuroplasticity. Think back to "the neurons that fire together wire together." In short, if you practice something every day, those skills become part of the structure and function of your brain.

Replacing negative thoughts with a positive self-concept will lead to more positive outcomes. You will also have the added benefits of a growth mind-set, the understanding that the more you apply these skills, the more motivation you can unleash. On a very fundamental level, the idea that you can boost your motivation empowers you to keep looking for solutions to get to your goals. Some of these tools may work for you, some may not. The outcomes you get are dependent on your one-of-a-kind personality. If you find a handful of tools that work for you, you can begin to see progress, which itself will motivate you.

Dr. Lara Says

The label "unmotivated" can become like a virus that disrupts a computer's performance and causes crashes. For teens who have a diagnosis such as ADHD or another executive dysfunction, these negative labels can impact their sense of identity and all the different actions that they're willing to take or not willing to take. Motivation is a super skill you can build—new skills create new neural connections.

Positive Self-Talk

Tell yourself, *I can increase my motivation by being encouraging rather than discouraging to myself.*

Motivational Enhancement—Finding Your Own Inner Compass

Deep down you know you want to make some changes. Barriers to that change may be fear that you don't have what it takes, or an attitude of "Why try?" that can result from discouragement. There is a science to increasing motivation, and beyond that science is the poetry of your dreams, imagination, and desires. These can be your most potent guides to the lifelong process of self-discovery.

Psychologists William Miller and Stephen Rollnick (2012) developed an effective set of tools to help increase motivation by finding your own inner compass. These tools include (1) developing discrepancy, (2) supporting self-efficacy, (3) rolling with resistance, and (4) self-compassion. We'll cover all four in this chapter so that you can develop your super skill of motivation.

Developing Discrepancy

One way to increase motivation is to develop discrepancy, which means paying attention to the conflicts between what you are doing and what you want for yourself. What's important here is that you're not making changes because someone told you to; you are doing it because you want change for yourself. It is important to understand that it is absolutely not self-criticism. It is the opposite—a gentle approach to reminding yourself what you really want and realizing that your behaviors may be hurting you.

Developing discrepancy means noticing that a bad thing is a bad thing. If you walked into a room and saw a pile of garbage, you probably wouldn't think, *That garbage adds a little something special to the atmosphere.* You would hopefully be motivated to get rid of the garbage. It is easier to fool ourselves about our own habits than about something as obvious as garbage.

Developing discrepancy means getting real and knowing when something is good for you and when it's not. A simple example is that maybe getting notifications on your phone all day from every social media platform, app, text, and email is actually … wait for it … garbage. If you call it what it is, you can take control and go to your settings to limit how many notifications you get on your phone.

One way to think of developing discrepancy is to stop fooling yourself about the costs of certain behaviors, such as vaping. The risks of vaping have made headlines for a lung disease that has resulted in deaths. Other risks include potential for addiction and creating conflict with your parents that will lead to consequences and restrictions on your freedom. It may seem that there are benefits to bonding with others or the high that results, but that same high from tobacco or marijuana may create a habit that is hard to break. Any use of a substance to manage mood or find focus limits your freedom, given the risk of becoming dependent on that substance. The six super skills can also solve some of the problems of managing mood and finding focus. The best way to stop fooling yourself is to make a list of all of the costs of a behavior, including its risks.

We will look closely at the example of procrastination because that is one of the biggest pain points, with the pressure many teens feel to do well in school. Procrastination may be a form of self-sabotage that prevents you from finding your true gifts. If you procrastinate on your writing assignments, your main focus becomes getting them done. If you allow yourself more time, you have the chance to develop your writing skills and discover a talent. Many people who discovered a talent for writing later in life were surprised because their procrastination habits in school had led them to think of writing as a punishing activity. Under stress, they weren't able to show their true capacity and get the encouragement they might have found if they had put in the time.

Action vs. Procrastination

Taking action and procrastination are two different paths that take you to two different end points. Instead of telling yourself, *I can always do this later*, you want to get real about the goals you will not attain if you procrastinate.

Procrastination in any area, whether it be extracurricular activities or sports, leads to worse results than action. Motivation is the fuel generated by increasing your awareness of the massive gap between the outcomes of action versus procrastination.

• *Riya's Story*

Riya wanted to get a role in the next high school performance. She considered signing up for an improv class to help her with the audition and build her comfort on stage. She thought about how nervous she would be in an improv class and started to back out. When she realized that she would be more likely to get the part if she took the class, she compared the disappointment of not getting a role and feeling left out by her friends who had parts to the exhilaration of being in the play and letting her talent shine. She decided to take the class.

The Costs of Procrastination

If you had a senior project due in one month and you started today and finished it early, you would not have to worry about it for twenty-nine days. If you procrastinated, you would be worrying about it every day that you did not do it. The cost here is constant worry.

We have only so much bandwidth to handle all our different demands. If some of that bandwidth is taken up by worrying about things that you could start but choose not to, you are decreasing your efficiency. Think about doing focused work on your computer when you have one tab up compared to having fifteen tabs up. Focus comes easier without the pull of so many options in plain view. Spending a big chunk of your time worrying about all the projects hanging over your head interferes with your focus and attention. Completing one project will free you up to turn your attention to other goals or the next step in one goal. Procrastination can also cause you to miss opportunities.

TRY IT   Think of a project that is weighing on your mind. Take out your journal or Notes app, and list all the pros and cons of procrastination you can think of for a specific project. As an example of a pro, some people think that procrastination shows you what your priorities are in the sense that if you really cared about something you would do it; one of the cons of procrastination is having to stress about your project for all the time you do not get started. What other pros and cons can you think of?

Stress: A Major Cost of Procrastination

Procrastination keeps you from the things you want because it is an indefinite drain on your mental bandwidth. If you procrastinate enough, taking action can become doubly difficult because of stress.

The longer you put something off, the more stressful the task becomes as the deadline looms. Your body releases stress hormones that make it harder to pay attention to the work at hand. Your heart may be racing, your breathing shallow, your muscles tense, all interfering with concentration. All this can be avoided by starting a project when you get an assignment, even if only to write a time-line for completion.

• *Vince's Story*

As a serious astronomy geek, Vince was very excited about the upcoming total solar eclipse. The eclipse would be visible across a span of the United States from coast to coast. He knew he had to purchase a pair of viewing glasses because he could damage his eyes if he looked at the eclipse directly. Unfortunately, he waited until a few days before the eclipse and was unable to buy any viewing glasses. All the local stores were sold out, and he couldn't get any delivered in time. For Vince, the day of the eclipse was darkened by the stress caused by how to view it without the appropriate eye gear.

Have you ever missed an incredible opportunity because you procrastinated?

Focus on the Benefits of Completion

We have to do our absolute best to visualize the rewards of completion. Why are we doing what we're doing? What's the point? It goes back to the purpose of the goal. Is it a feeling? Is it something physical? Tangible?

Think of something you have been putting off. What feelings do you get when you visualize the rewards of completing this project? Will you get an overwhelming sense of relief or pride? Will you get something tangible, like a paycheck if you get yourself a summer job? Will you gain physical fitness if you check off going to the gym for the day?

The main idea here is that you can increase motivation by developing discrepancy between taking action and procrastination. The result of looking at benefits and costs of procrastination is that you can call yourself out for fooling yourself that whatever you have to do will be easier at a later time.

Self-Efficacy

Self-efficacy is the belief that you are capable of succeeding at specific tasks with effort. It can be a guiding image of who you are that is positive, capable, and resilient. Self-efficacy has been shown to improve grades, physical activity, health outcomes, and overall satisfaction with life. Self-efficacy can protect against depression, which is defined by a persistent, internal, global negative view of the self.

Imagine you are a football player in the state championship game. It is fourth down, and you have inches to move the ball to get a first down. Your coach tells you to go for the first down. You have been here before, and you know what you have to do. It's not easy. Remembering all the times you have gotten that first down helps you stay focused and determined. You block out self-doubt—and you get your first down!

NEWS FLASH! We interrupt this book for a public service announcement: concussions in football may pose risks to executive functioning.

Beyond the potential risk, what this example shows is that focusing on previous successes is a formula for increasing task-specific confidence.

One of the biggest barriers to being motivated is self-doubt. We know we should get around to doing what we should be doing. So why do we wait? What holds us back? If it's good for us, why don't we just go do it? Sometimes you are afraid you just won't measure up. Notice how unmotivated you feel if you say to yourself, *Why should I prepare for this speech when I'm not going to be good at it and I might get some bad feedback that I don't really want to hear?*

The importance of managing self-doubt is why the first super skill is finding gifts. When you begin to be filled with doubt, you need to remember your track record. Life isn't going to be a graph of constant growth. You may grow for a while, but you can't grow forever. No company stays on top forever. No athlete. No country. Just look at a stock ticker. Pick any great company you see or hear about on the news. Amazon. Google. Apple. You name it, that company has had ups, and that company has had downs. Why did investors continue to put their faith in these companies? Because they saw their track records of previous successes. So when you're down in the dumps, fall back on your past successes. Remind yourself that you've come this far, and that you can go a little further. And hey, quit being so hard on yourself!

TRY IT   Using your Notes app or journal, create a list of your past successes. Ask friends and family for reminders of successes. Review this list any time you are filled with self-doubt.

One time at a book signing, a young woman came up to me crying. She told me that it had taken her many years to discover the theme of one of my books—that ADHD can be a gift. She had struggled with many school failures. Her story was ultimately a success story. She did eventually graduate with a degree from a university. The secret to her transformation was that she learned that the further she went in her education, the more she could take classes that were really interesting to her. She learned that she had a special talent for generating original perspectives. Whereas in high school she had to be a good studier, in college she could get good grades on opinion papers where her originality stood out. She had to shift her self-concept from believing that ADHD meant she couldn't be a good student to knowing that she had many talents and interests that could fuel her success.

So, the easiest way to create a sense of self-efficacy is to just list your past successes! This will remind you of how capable you truly are, which is motivating.

Rolling with Resistance

Resistance is that sense of "not feeling like it." Rolling with resistance means that you stay nonjudgmental and accepting of yourself even when you feel unmotivated. If you feel backed into a corner when you feel pressure to get started, rolling with resistance will give you a choice. You can remind yourself that you are free to choose to start now or to plan to start in a half hour. Just for fun, when you don't feel like doing your homework, ask yourself, *What are the benefits of not doing my homework?* Rather than getting defensive, you are honoring your feeling and are open to the idea that there are reasons for that feeling. It's kind of funny only because in most cases there are few benefits to avoiding homework, but the willingness to explore benefits can create an openness to move forward.

When we find ourselves not wanting to study for a test or practice piano or just get up off the couch, our resistance can feel like a wall that seems immovable or too high to get over. Many of us have an automatic response to resistance: we let it win! It can be a learned behavior, a neuropathway we have traveled too many times, but it is also one we can change. Part of rolling with resistance is to notice it and label it without giving in to it. Think of a positive vision of you being motivated and driven. Imagine a cheerleader reminding you that you have what it takes.

You can change the message you give yourself about resistance. Think of motivation as an exotic flower that has to be cultivated. Under harsh conditions, it will fade. Trying to steamroll your resistance—for example, by telling yourself you're lazy or raising the bar higher and higher—will decrease your motivation. Negative labels can become self-fulfilling, and they can bring down your mood, which interferes with attention.

Positive Self-Talk

Tell yourself, *I can do this. Just get started and I'll gain some momentum.*

Or: *I have everything it takes to get my goals.*

Rolling with Resistance Means Getting Real

Instead of beating yourself up when you feel tempted to procrastinate, try telling yourself to get real. Procrastination is so tempting because it is immediately rewarded. If you have to do something hard and you let yourself off the hook, you are immediately rewarded with the relief of not having to focus hard, dig into math problems, or put on your jogging shoes.

Because it's so easy to fool ourselves that we will get it done "sometime, just not now," we do not always see that there are high costs to procrastination.

Positive Self-Talk

Tell yourself, *I am not going to fool myself that avoiding this hard task makes life easier. In the long run, it makes life harder.*

Feel the Resistance and Do It Anyway

When you feel resistance to studying for your exams, starting that science project, or running the mile, you don't need to psychoanalyze yourself to figure out why. The answer is actually really simple. These things are all very hard, so of course there's a part of you that wants to put them off! Instead of trying to figure out why you resist, start a habit where you say to yourself, *Every time I say I don't feel like it, I postpone goal getting.* It's as simple as that.

Think of feeling the resistance and doing it anyway as like lifting weights; just because it's hard to do doesn't mean you don't do it. This same tough attitude is required for military training where the expression "embrace the suck" is used as a reminder that hard things aren't a signal to run away, but rather a challenge to you to rise to the occasion. Imagine two pathways that are open to you in that moment when you are tempted to delay getting started on your homework to check out Snapchat: you can (1) think about how much easier it would be to pick up your phone, or (2) use the temptation to fuel your determination to defeat your own resistance and get started.

Positive Self-Talk

Tell yourself, *I can do hard things.*

Or: *I will review my goal list as a reminder of how important this is to me.*

Self-Compassion

You can also decrease resistance by talking to yourself the way you would talk to your best friend, with kindness, encouragement, and self-compassion, the fourth tool to help increase motivation.

Self-compassion may mean admitting that there are many paths to success, and your path may not look like everyone else's. Not everyone has to get straight As to accomplish their goals. For those with more severe challenges, just graduating from high school is a significant accomplishment, and they will need to call on many of the super skills to achieve this.

Self-compassion can help you be easier on yourself if you set realistic goals. Maybe you're being too hard on yourself. By stepping outside of your life, your shell, your current situation, you can gain new perspective. Maybe you do this through taking a break, meditating, or talking to someone who cares about you. Whatever you do to gain new perspective on your experience, keep in mind a goal of gaining a better grasp of your current state.

Think Differently about Thinking Differently: Neurodiversity

One idea that strengthens self-compassion is the idea of *neurodiversity*; instead of thinking of executive dysfunction as a brain disorder, think of it as a brain difference. Neurodiversity means that our brain differences are predictable variations and are part of all that makes us unique human beings. Just as we differ in race, culture, height, and religion, so too do we differ in in how our brains work. School systems may not go far enough to address the reality that there are all kinds of minds. Being a human can be painful, and we are all so different, yet we all want to feel like we belong. Self-compassion can stop a cycle of increasing self-doubt.

It's common for students to get sent to the principal's office for talking too much in class. Self-compassion in that case means realizing that the "gift of gab" may create problems in school but in many career choices will be a major asset. Areas such as social media marketing, sales, customer service, politics, or teaching offer jobs where the gift of gab can make people feel welcome and relaxed. The compassion may be to recognize that the very same natural talents that can lead to success are not appreciated in school settings and to hold out for the time where you can use them as necessary skills.

How Can You Make This More Fun?

While you can get in trouble for trying to have some fun in the classroom, another tool for increasing motivation is to find ways to make things more fun! Ironic, isn't it?

Fun is the opposite of resistance. Fun makes us chase after activities with anticipation. Fun will allow you to tap into the enjoyment aspect of setting goals. Fun shifts your focus to the process, as opposed to the goal itself. You can make the journey to the goal as fun as possible. The more fun you make the journey, the more motivated you will be. For example, there are many different routes you could take to the mall. You could just hop on the highway and go the quickest way, but that may be the most boring. What about the scenic route? Yes, it may be slower, but you're going to enjoy the process a whole lot more.

When it comes to goals, enjoy the process. Life isn't all about goals. Most of the time, it's about the process.

Ninety-nine percent of the process of achieving goals occurs during the part when we are not actually celebrating having achieved the goal. Let's say you take AP Chemistry because you want to be a doctor. How can that be fun? You are part of a greater ecosystem of purpose, whether you know it or not. You have value, just as studying for that chemistry test has value. It will propel you to becoming a doctor, to diagnosing patients and helping them feel better, or conducting research that will change lives.

You might look back and think, *I wish I had enjoyed the ride a little more.* If you get too caught up in the end result, you'll miss all the great things happening along the way.

One great way to make things more fun is to find social support. Finding a group can create a lot of motivation and momentum. For example, to make exercise more fun, Elena tells herself, *I pay more for scheduled fitness classes, but at least I tend to procrastinate less about going because I'm "in the trenches" with other people, bonding through hardship and making friends.*

Value Rest and Play

Another way to maintain a steady level of motivation is to value rest and play. Rest is different from procrastination because it is in the service of restoration, not delay. Play can also restore a positive mood, bringing a sense of refreshment that will help increase energy to take on your work. Unlike rest and play, procrastination can create tension because you know you are avoiding doing something that needs to be done.

There are times when that sense of "I just don't feel like it" is a reflection of being burned out or depleted. If you feel that way, you're not alone. Stress is taking a major toll on teenagers these days. Often the demands are too intense, and many parents and teens have lost perspective on the balance that is required for mental and physical health.

You may have signed up for three leadership positions to try to boost your college application, but this may be a win-lose situation. If you make so many commitments that you don't get enough sleep, and a balance of social activities and downtime, you can be setting yourself up for depression or anxiety.

Rest is important not only for mental and physical health but also for recharging the brain. You are not a machine; if you keep pushing yourself, you create stress, tense muscles, and loss of perspective. Rest can range from napping, lying at the pool, "doing nothing," or puttering around with no goal in mind. Other restorative activities include wandering in natural settings, coloring books (not just for kids anymore), drawing, or playing with your pet. Even a daily practice of appreciating what is can restore energy.

Play is different from rest in that it involves activity for the purpose of recreation, whereas rest is taking a break from activity. Play means activity that can involve imagination and by definition is not high stakes or stressful. Rest can restore your mind and body, whereas play can boost your mood, help you feel more connected to others, improve your sense of humor, and energize you. Some examples of play include:

- playing pick-up sports (whether you play to win or just to enjoy good friends) or actively cheering for your favorite team

- taking on the dungeon master role in Dungeons and Dragons

- hosting a group to sample your favorite salsas and chips

- dancing to music in your own room

TRY IT Using your journal or Notes app, write down a list of five activities that feel like play for you.

Look at How Far You Have Come

Imagine you are climbing up a huge mountain and you always notice how far you have to go, but you never turn around and look at how far you've come. That can make it hard to stay motivated. Now imagine you take a look back and see how far you have already come. For many people, that increases motivation because they see how their hard work has paid off. Seeing how far you've come requires flexible thinking. It is all-or-nothing thinking to look at a challenge and only notice the parts of it that are hard or the parts of yourself that are lacking. For every challenge, there are also parts that are easy and specific strengths that prepare you for the challenge.

Seek Progress, Not Perfection

Some psychologists say that perfectionism can turn into self-abuse, if no matter how much you achieve it's never good enough. What's worse, it often backfires. For example, one study found that "perfectionism is strongly and consistently related to numerous 'detrimental' work and nonwork outcomes, including higher levels of burnout, stress, workaholism, anxiety, and depression" (Swider et al. 2018). Perfectionism looks for the gap between where you are and how far you have to go to get to perfection—a state that is not realistically attainable. The problem is that it overlooks all the progress that can be a source of motivation to keep going. Looking at progress is encouraging and keeps you going for the long haul.

Perfectionism may also look at others who are ahead of you and create deep insecurities and unrelenting pressure to be the best. I hope you don't take that to mean you should set small goals or lose confidence in yourself. The problem with perfectionism is that it tends to skip over the super skills of finding gifts, setting goals, and chunking those goals down into smaller steps. Even when you have set a landmark ahead and have noticed how far you have come, you can still remember to enjoy the ride.

• *Anne's Story*

Anne walked out of her geometry final feeling totally wrecked. She had studied hard and knew math was not her strength, but she didn't expect to do so poorly on it. She cried at the frustration she felt for having tried so hard and still struggling so much. She started to think, Why should I even study if it doesn't pay off?

When she talked with her dad about it, he said, "Everyone has an Achilles' heel." As usual, Anne rolled her eyes at her dad's weird remarks. He went on to explain that Achilles was a mythological Greek god whose mother made him immortal by dipping him into a river. Because she was holding him by the heels, that was the only place he could be killed. Her dad said that everyone has a weak spot, and while Anne might consider using the student tutoring center, she shouldn't let her confidence and motivation be crushed by a hard test in an area that was especially challenging for her.

Motivation is like any skill—the more you practice, the better you get. If you practice shooting, passing, and dribbling every day, you get better at playing basketball. Or think of bodybuilders. If they go to the gym every day, they can look strong even if they have naturally small builds. So too the super skill of motivation can become part of the function and structure of your brain; you can become a mind builder and create strength in motivation.

CHAPTER 6

Managing Mood

Tell the negative committee that meets inside your head to sit down and shut up.

—Ann Bradford

The Buddha says, "Life is suffering," but we are surrounded by social media images that suggest otherwise. A positive reframe of Buddha's wisdom is not that life is suffering, but rather that "work is life," which offers the hope that the work of executive functioning can spare you some suffering. This doesn't mean work is more important than relationships or having fun, but that both fun and good relationships require work. It requires work not to criticize those we love but rather to pause to think of an encouraging comment.

We humans evolved to survive, not to have fun. Over time, we developed systems that help us survive by reducing surprise and predicting possible encounters with threats (Mobbs et al. 2015). One way to reduce surprise is to constantly predict bad things that can happen and mentally rehearse strategies to increase life expectancy. In short, evolution supported fearful reactions and negative rehearsal; our nervous systems evolved to be nervous.

Distressing emotions capture your attention, derailing you from focus. This may be why 33 percent of children with ADHD have an anxiety disorder and 17 percent struggle with depression (Danielson et al. 2018). Because having an impairment in attention (ADHD) makes it harder for you to control your negative emotions, this super skill is so important; managing your mood will improve your attention.

This chapter will give you a set of tools to turn the dial toward happiness. If you've been paying attention, you will know by now that how you talk to yourself is going to be a big part of how you can manage your mood.

Flexible Thinking

It's easy to get caught up in your own thoughts. Just as our minds can be infinitely candid, they can be equally deceptive. Our perception of reality is concocted in our minds and our minds alone. In difficult situations, you can choose to look for the positives. Doing this is hard work and easier said than done, but it is worth it. We all know people who manage to keep their heads up when having a hard time, as well as other people who seem to have it all, yet still find a lot to complain about. We all have good and bad things in our lives; a lot of how we respond, and how we feel, comes down to where we choose to focus our attention. Sometimes our minds play tricks on us. They tell us that we can't go on. That we should give up. There are many pathways to not letting our minds drag us down.

Flexible thinking is a powerful tool you can use to regulate your emotions and learn to focus on positive self-talk. Self-talk is like having a helpful coach or a supportive cheerleader inside your own mind. By coaching yourself, you can create stable confidence that doesn't move wildly depending on the predictable ups and downs of life. For example, if you saw your friends posting party photos on Instagram and you were not invited, it would be easy to spiral down into self-doubt and think things like, *They don't like me* or *I don't have any friends.*

Dr. Lara Says

Flexible thinking means looking for many different ways of seeing a situation that are not going to cause you to think there is something wrong with you. Flexible thinking allows you to stay less reactive through all the drama of the teenage years. It also helps you stay confident in the face of challenging situations.

If you find yourself feeling left out, here are some things you can think about:

- *Are these my only friends? Who else am I friends with?*

- *Have they included me in past events?*

- *Are there reasons I wasn't invited that have nothing to do with them rejecting me?* (For example, did they all finish studying for a class they take together and go out afterward without inviting people who were not in the class?)

- *I know some people in that group are jealous of me. Maybe that's why I wasn't invited, but that doesn't mean there's something wrong with me.*

- *I know some people think I'm too bossy, but I have other friends who like that I take charge. I can't change my main attributes, but I can try to be more flexible.*

- *How can I make new friends?*

TRY IT   Think of additional responses to this situation of feeling left out and write them in your journal or Notes app section on super skills.

The opposite of flexible thinking is catastrophic thinking—narrowing in on the worst possible explanation for events. When you find yourself catastrophizing, label the thought "catastrophizing" so you don't buy into it. Then you can go through the questions above and practice flexible thinking, finding more positive thoughts and courses of action. By labeling the catastrophic thinking, you can gain distance from it and not take it so seriously. Once you have labeled it, you can ask yourself, *Is it true?* You will often find that you are using all-or nothing thinking: you think you weren't invited because people don't like you, but more often they were caught up in the moment. Search for reasons to help you manage the situation. You can tell yourself, *I am more than capable of finding solutions.* Be creative by thinking of ways that a disappointment is not the end of the story. Be as kind to yourself as you would be to a friend you cared about.

Pausing

Another powerful tool to help you regulate your emotions is the power of the pause. We all get caught up in the swing of things. We're going so fast and so hard that we forget where we are. When this happens, it's easy to get carried away by our emotions. As in the earlier example, if you see your friends posting on Instagram and you feel left out, you might let your mind go to darker and darker places, like believing that you were left out because you have so many flaws that no one could possibly want to be your friend.

In situations when you are tempted to take impulsive action or go down dark mental alleys, you can tell yourself, *Pause.* In that moment, you can try these approaches:

- Put your feelings into words. The more precise the language you can find, the easier it will be to find a solution to what's troubling you.

- Redirect your behavior to get some space from the situation and your thoughts and feelings. It could be as simple as calling someone who cares about you or going for a walk.

- Focus on your personal goals for the future. Reviewing your goals can pull you out of the immediate emotional pain to find hope. Focusing on your goals reminds you that you can control your life.

It's important to note that pausing is completely different from stopping. Pausing helps you get a handle on your emotional reactions before acting, whereas stopping means sweeping your emotions under the rug. When we pause, we're just taking a siesta, or a brief hiatus to refocus. Perhaps we physically, mentally, or emotionally need a break, or maybe we need to reevaluate why we're doing what we're doing. The point is that a pause should have purpose.

Some teens might feel like they need to turn to drugs or alcohol to take a break. Using drugs and alcohol are impulsive behaviors themselves and also encourage other impulsive behavior. Over time, impulsive behavior can become mindless or automatic. You reach for a harmful substance instead of learning to soothe yourself. Putting a pause in between craving and an impulsive action allows you to think of other super skills that will help you not just avoid an impulsive reaction but also respond in a way that actually makes a situation better.

There's a Super Skill for That!

Let's take a quick look back (and ahead):

- Have you had a blow to your confidence? Did you get a C in a class you expected to get a B in? Using the super skill finding gifts, remind yourself of your enduring talents. Write down a list of times you felt appreciated in the last week.

- Are you overwhelmed by a large project that is creating a lot of anxiety? Think about chunking. What's the smallest piece of it that seems manageable? Get started, and create a plan with a time for work and a time for a break.

- Do you feel unmotivated to get started on studying for your SAT? Remind yourself of the costs of not studying and the benefits of studying. That's the super skill of boosting motivation in chapter 5.

- You want to relax? Okay, there's a super skill for that—finding focus. A powerful way to calm yourself down is through deep breathing. You'll learn more about that in the next chapter.

You can see how simply taking a pause and adding some positive self-talk can help you manage your emotions through using all the other super skills.

The Language of Emotions

Here's a fun fact: the more precise the language you use to describe your emotions, the less likely you are to use a substance to manage your emotions (Kashdan et al. 2010). So the next time you are struggling with a negative emotion, name the feeling, google synonyms for it, and review the list of alternate words. Select the one that best matches your feelings and situation. For example, the *Merriam-Webster* dictionary offers the following for synonyms of "sad": blue, brokenhearted, cast down, crestfallen, dejected, depressed, despondent, disconsolate, doleful, down, downcast, downhearted, down in the mouth, droopy, forlorn, gloomy, glum, hangdog, heartbroken, heartsick, heartsore, heavyhearted, inconsolable, joyless, low, low-spirited, melancholic, melancholy, miserable, mournful, saddened, sorrowful, sorry, unhappy, woebegone, woeful, wretched.

Instead of trying to get rid of the feeling of sadness, be willing to experience it. Be willing to be curious about it and explore what words more precisely describe what you are going through. Failure and disappointments are going to be part of life, and managing mood is the process of getting back up. Emotions are communications to ourselves, from ourselves, about ourselves. Managing mood does not mean getting rid of painful emotions. There are many costs to repressing emotions. Research shows us that it's not easy to avoid emotions, and it creates tension to try to do so. Avoiding emotions also creates relationship problems (Johnson 2010). Emotions can guide our communication with others about how their behavior impacts us.

• *Jack's Story*

Jack went to a party and sat next to a girl he had a crush on. He tried to get her attention, but she walked away soon after he sat down. He felt humiliated. Instead of drinking away his feeling of humiliation with alcohol, he let himself feel the sting of rejection. He realized that she hadn't even smiled at him, and that although she may have wanted to get away from him, she was a person who couldn't even be friendly. He told himself he wouldn't be interested in someone who wasn't kind anyway. Noticing some friends across the room, he moved on to talk with them. He was able to give himself credit for taking the risk of approaching her and remembered what his father liked to say: "If you ask ten girls out for Saturday night and only one says yes, you still have a date on Saturday night."

Managing Anger

Anger is one of the most potent and therefore difficult-to-manage emotions. You will want to try pausing and flexible thinking when managing your anger. It's also important to admit when you're angry and to communicate that in healthy ways. If you suppress your anger, it can become a landmine. As psychologists like to say, "If you don't talk about it, you're going to act it out." Being able to identify anger, manage it, and communicate assertively when appropriate are vital life skills.

These two additional ideas can help you manage your anger:

- Admit when you're angry. Anger may mean there is a deeper conflict you have to sort out. Anger is signaling you—pause, pay attention, don't move past this too quickly.

- Imagine a wand moving very slowly from the top of your head down to your toes, looking for any hot spots of anger, physical tension, or pain. When you find a hot spot, describe the physical sensation you are experiencing. You can be creative and come up with a vivid image. Does it feel like a fire, a stabbing pain, an unmovable rock? Describe the sensation as carefully as you can. This process allows you to get a handle on the emotion.

When you feel angry, it's important to pause and think carefully about whether it's appropriate to communicate your anger with the person who has made you angry. One strategy that a lot of people use is to find a neutral person to talk to and get their perspective and advice. In addition to helping you cool down, this strategy can help you rehearse what you want to say beforehand to make sure that you will share your feelings in a way the other person can understand.

If you decide to have a conversation with the person, one of the most important tips for success is to use *I-messages* rather than *you-messages*. As an example, you would say, "I am hurt and angry that you made fun of my stuttering when I gave my talk in class," rather than, "You purposely embarrassed me in class by making fun of me." When you use an I-message, you accept responsibility for your role. In contrast, using a you-message means you are creating an explanation for a motive that you can't really know for sure. You will also want to give the other person a chance to respond, and be sure to listen as closely as you can. If you want, you can let them know you hear them, even if that means "parroting" or repeating back to them what you heard. The strategy of repeating what the other person said involves both a pause and flexible thinking. In the time it takes to repeat back what you heard, you are gaining some time to collect yourself, and by taking seriously the other person's perspective, you are using flexible thinking.

Positive Self-Talk

When you feel angry, tell yourself, *I am calm. I am focused.*

Or: *I can take a few deep breaths before I take action.*

Or: *I can find someone to talk to before I take action.*

Dr. Lara Says

Some people may be given the message that they need to be cheerful all the time. What we know about managing mood is that unexpressed and unheard anger can lead to depression. What you are feeling has important information for you.

When you feel angry, the simplest step you can take is to label the feeling "anger." Just by putting a label on it, you gain some distance and more control over your behavior. This one simple step is a game changer—it allows you to have the emotion rather than to be the emotion.

• *Brandie's Story*

Brandie worried a lot about her dad. Often, when she came home from school, she could tell he had been smoking weed. She was angry that her dad wouldn't stop smoking. One of her friends told her that when her dad drove them to the movies last weekend, she smelled weed in the car. Her friend told her mom, who said she couldn't drive with Brandie anymore. Not only was Brandie worried about her dad but she also felt ashamed that her friends could smell the weed in the car.

Brandie set up an appointment to ask the school counselor for help. The counselor asked her to write down all her feelings about her dad. She listed the feelings of worry, shame, and anger. Her counselor told her, "You can't control or cure your dad's smoking, and you are not the cause of it."

When Brandie went home after the session, she practiced the mindfulness tool her therapist had given her: staying with one feeling at a time and focusing on her breath while she labeled the feeling. Brandie was still really mad at her dad, but after practicing the writing and mindfulness, she was able to focus on getting her schoolwork done. She found a way to feel the anger, but not let it distract her from her goals.

Translating Complaints into Requests

Another mood management tool is to turn a complaint into a request. Whenever you come to a roadblock, don't complain that it's there. Rather, try to do everything within your power and abilities to overcome it. You may need help. If you do, figure out exactly what the problem is, identify the best person or people to help you overcome it, and then ask for the help you need.

To help you figure out what specific request you want to make, you first need to identify the underlying feeling within the complaint. For example, if your complaint is that your parents nag you to take care of chores when you get home from school, you may be feeling overwhelmed by all the different things you have to do. In this case, instead of complaining that they won't get off your back, you can calmly give some of the good reasons you need to take a break between school and starting homework. In person or by text, you can request that there be a "no nagging" time the first hour after school because you have a lot on your mind and need to decompress.

If you want to get even better at translating complaints into requests, you can practice using an I-message with a parent. You could say something like, "It increases my anxiety to have you worry so much. I need to figure this out for myself. I'm going to be going away to college in two years." You could even request that a parent listen to what you're worried about rather than sharing their own worries, which adds fuel to the fire. You might also ask to have time together that is just for bonding, with no talk about grades or college or chores that need to be done around the house.

Every time you notice yourself with a complaint about a teacher, a friend, a parent, or a coach, try to identify the feeling underneath it and ask yourself what specific request you can make to that person. You can request that the person listen to what you're feeling rather than trying to solve the problem for you. You can request that a friend not tell others about your family problems. Making specific requests is not only a way to manage your moods but also a way to solve specific problems.

Reducing Stress by Taking a Broader Perspective

We lose control of our emotions when we lose perspective on a situation. Imagine yourself in a plane at thirty thousand feet or zooming out the camera lens; you're able to notice things that you may have not been able to notice before. Imagine a current situation as a camera lens. If you zoom out, you'll see that there is so much more in the picture frame than you initially thought.

Stress was not meant to be a chronic mode of operation, particularly for developing brains. Toxic stress disrupts physical and mental health, and the earlier that chronic stress hits the developing brain, the greater the risks to long-term health. Tolerable stress is comparatively infrequent, allowing the brain to recover. Frequent prolonged stress can negatively impact the architecture of the brain, creating lifelong mental health risks (National Scientific Council on the Developing Child 2005/2014).

Recent research has led to the conclusion that there is "an urgent need to help students reduce their experience of overwhelming levels of stress during college" (Liu et al. 2019). This study found that:

- Stress exposure was strongly associated with mental health diagnoses, self-harm, and suicidality.

- Twenty-five percent of students reported being diagnosed with or treated for a mental health disorder in the prior year.

119

- Twenty percent of all students surveyed had thought about suicide, with 9 percent reporting having attempted suicide and nearly 20 percent reporting self-injury.

With a broader perspective, you can learn to regulate your emotions and moderate toxic stress.

Detachment: Taking the Passenger Seat in Your College Search

One of the biggest issues where it is easy to lose perspective—and increase stress as a result—is in planning for college. For example, applying to a dozen or more schools, while expecting catastrophe if you don't get into an elite school, is a formula for chronic stress. Every quiz, test, and project will affect your brain in the same way an attacking lion geared up our ancestors' brains to escape.

For college seekers, the first step is to take a broader perspective and increase detachment in college choice. Detachment is by definition a way to take the emotion out of a situation. It does not imply lowering one's standards, but rather attaining nonreactivity about the outcome—recognizing that whatever college you attend, there will be advantages and disadvantages. The more selective a college is, the more resources and elite network you will have access to, but also the more competition and stress you will face.

Think of the difference between driving a car and being a passenger. When you're driving, you have to stay narrowly focused on the road ahead and may miss the bigger picture: the beautiful Rocky Mountains, for example. You may scream at other drivers because you're navigating a treacherous curve. You've got your feet switching back and forth between the brake and the gas pedal, your eyes are looking for cars ahead and behind, and simultaneously you're keeping the car in its lane. As a passenger, however, you don't have much to worry about. Picture yourself in the passenger seat, able to take in the snow-covered peaks of the Rockies or the mountain goats scaling the cliffs above you. You can observe these details because you are not preoccupied by driving the car.

A broader perspective also allows you to look around and see how fortunate you are to have so many choices for college, and to be grateful for how far you have come. In college, you will have more opportunity to pursue coursework in your special interests. The increased relevance of your classes will boost your motivation. And you will likely have more time to yourself than in high school, because you will be spending less time in the classroom.

Perhaps your dream school means your competition will be tougher, so you will be more stressed and may lose confidence. You may also have to take out more student loans. Your safe school may have less access to an elite network but give you a chance to build your confidence by having less competition. Even your fallback school may have many benefits, including decreased stress once you are a student, or a particular specialization or professor you are eager to do research with.

TRY IT Using your Notes app or journal, list your dream school, your safe school, and a fallback school. Write down the benefits and costs of each option.

You don't have to have 100 percent positive self-talk to be happy. Negative emotions are healthy reactions to real life challenges and often contain guidance for you. You simply have to take some of the negative emotions and use these tools to create an increased balance of positive emotions to negative emotions.

CHAPTER 7

Finding Focus

To pay attention, this is our endless and proper work.

—Mary Oliver

When most people think of attention spans in today's digitized age, they think of how shortened they are, and the incredible number of distractions that are available to us each and every day, most of which come from the supercomputers that live in the depths of our pockets, purses, and handbags. Think about just how many notifications you receive every day, from texts to calls to Facebook to Instagram to Snapchat to email.

Some of you are so used to receiving texts and notifications that your brain is trained to think you should check your phone every five minutes, even if just to light up the screen to see that another five minutes has passed and that you didn't miss a message by mistake.

Controlling your attention is a practice. In addition to choosing what to focus on, you have to choose what to filter out. Once you have chosen where to put your attention, your task is to concentrate on the single task at hand. This task may have multiple pieces, come in different parts, and be completed over the course of different time spans. The most important thing to note is that your concentration is on this specific task, not the one before, not the one after.

It's also significant to note the effect of distractions on attention. Perhaps we are inclined to move away from our current objectives because we know that another one is easier, or we start to put it off, thinking that we can do it later. Tuning out distractions is as important as dialing in on the chosen task. This chapter will give you eight research-backed tools for boosting your attention. You can also remember that the super skill of chunking can help you select one small task at a time and goal setting can help you figure out what is a priority.

You don't have to memorize or master all eight tools. Choose three that are the easiest for you to experiment with, and give them a try. Many of these tools have multiple benefits, including for your physical health, managing mood, and confidence.

The idea that attention can be improved by lifestyle choices can help you develop a growth mind-set toward attention. The harder you try, the more of these attention boosters you use, the more you can increase your attention.

Exercise

In his book *Spark: The Revolutionary New Science of Exercise and the Brain*, John Ratey emphasizes the point that exercise has one of the most powerful abilities to increase attention. In his

2018 TEDX Talk, he said that exercise has the same effect on the brain as a bit of Adderall and a bit of Prozac. It both increases attention and improves mood.

An important point to remember is that simple exercises that boost your brain don't need to be of the same duration and intensity that it takes to get in physical shape. Short walks and bouncing a ball against a wall can boost attention, but it would likely take more exercise to get physically fit. Research has shown that even just fidgeting improved accuracy for students with ADHD (Hartanto et al. 2016). Hyperactivity—while considered a symptom—serves a purposeful function to increase cognitive performance.

A review of the research on exercise and the brain shows not only temporary boosts in attention but also brain changes over time. "Many studies have suggested that the parts of the brain that control thinking and memory (the prefrontal cortex and medial temporal cortex) have greater volume in people who exercise versus people who don't" (Godman 2018).

A 2015 study found that physical activity before school improved attention (Hoza et al. 2015). This finding leads to a simple recommendation about how you get to school. Is your school close enough to walk or bike to? If a parent has the time in the morning, a bike ride with your parent could be a fun bonding time while boosting your brain. Or what if you got dropped off at a place that required you to walk for five or ten minutes to get to school? You could avoid all the traffic heading to school and boost your brain at the same time.

Another way to apply this approach is when you're doing your homework. When your attention is drifting, you can find something that's five minutes away, and walk there and back. Two other simple options for getting exercise include finding a YouTube exercise video and working out for fifteen minutes, and walking to a favorite hangout place such as a library or coffee shop after school to do homework there. The second option might also offer a benefit of mixing up your homework routine to make it less boring. Walking to the place you choose, studying for an hour, then walking home can create a routine or rhythm for your remaining assignments.

Breaks: Attention Restoration

Take a break, take a breather, or just pause for a second. These are all suggestions that people offer in an effort to help someone who is overworked, stressed out, tired, or perhaps just lost. Just as you take breaks between reps of lifting weights, so too does your attention need to restore itself.

In Daniel Pink's book *When: The Scientific Secrets of Perfect Timing* (2018), he notes the power of a ten- to twenty-minute nap for increasing productivity. He also reports that one of the most powerful brain hacks is drinking a cup of coffee before you take a fifteen-minute nap. That might seem counterintuitive; perhaps you're thinking, *Well, that caffeine is not going to let me take a nap*, but it will take about fifteen minutes for the caffeine to get into your system. So you'll get a boost from the nap, but you'll get a double jolt because the caffeine will kick in right as you wake up. A general recommendation is that you not drink caffeine in the afternoon or later in the day because it can disrupt sleep.

You may be thinking, *How do I take a nap in the middle of the school day?* One teen weighs in on this dilemma: "Twenty minutes of me sleeping on my arm in the library seemed to do wonders. Anything longer, and I felt groggy afterward. Anything shorter, and I didn't feel fully rested and would need to put my head back down."

As you do your homework in the evenings or on the weekends, you will want to create a pattern of studying and taking breaks. This means that you want to find out how long you can work efficiently. You may want to figure out what is a high-resistance and a low resistance task.

For example, someone who has to do some reading might find that they don't mind doing that for longer than if they have to memorize Spanish conjugations. Imagine the difference between doing something that comes the hardest to you versus something that you enjoy a lot more, such as a specific subject. For some people, it might be working fifteen minutes on high-resistance tasks and thirty minutes on low-resistance tasks. The more resistance you have to getting started, the more you can sustain your attention by creating a smaller chunk.

People have to find the best timing for themselves. You can experiment with trying out different study doses. Can you pay attention for twenty minutes? A half hour? An hour?

One of the tools that many teens find the most effective is to start by saying, *I'm just going to do this for two minutes.* This is a bit of a trick because many people will keep going once they get started. And that's the idea of task initiation in executive functioning: sometimes just getting started is the hardest part.

Even keeping at a task for only two minutes can all add up, leading to a sense of progress and boosting your mood by being able to tell yourself, *Well, I got something done.* Experiment with different strategies. For example, some people who have a half-hour project can start with a fifteen-minute dose, take a break or enjoy some sort of reward, and then put in another fifteen minutes.

Sleep

One of the biggest disrupters of executive functioning is getting less sleep than needed; for teens, this means nine hours each night. Neuropsychologists tell us that "scientists have uncovered amazing evidence that what your brain learns during the day is consolidated during sleep. That means that the more sleep you get, the better your brain will remember and understand what you learned that day" (Deak and Deak 2013).

Gabe, a sophomore in high school, learned this the hard way: "Sometimes you have to go on a little sleep, because sometimes life happens. Deadlines are moved, priorities change, emergencies happen. But, if it's possible to get a good night's sleep, do it. I used to think I could run on five to six hours a night and be just fine. I was, until I wasn't. I was overworked, exhausted, and constantly searching for the next cup of coffee, the next place I could take a ten-minute power nap. My school, as well as my relationships, and most importantly, my mental health, suffered from this. Think about sleep this way."

Positive Self-Talk

Tell yourself, *The biggest brain builder is sleep. Stay strong, put your technology away, and get some sleep!*

Sleep is also essential for being able to pay attention during the day. According to the Harvard Medical School Division of Sleep Medicine (2007), "Sleep deprivation negatively impacts our mood, our ability to focus, and our ability to access higher-level cognitive functions. The combination of these factors is what we generally refer to as mental performance."

Technology can disrupt sleep. We have had an explosion of technology in recent years, beginning with the invention of the iPhone. The ability to watch TV shows and movies, and to access social media on our phones, can be addictive—and is also disruptive to sleep. It is recommended that you not read or watch TV in your bed to help you associate your bed with sleep and not other activities.

One recommended tool for helping you get to sleep is to dim bright lights an hour before bedtime—that means no technology one hour before bed. Our brains evolved to go to sleep when the sun went down, and since the invention of the light bulb and now smartphones, our natural biological processes for sleep have been disrupted.

One of the most powerful tools you can use to help you sleep is stress management before bedtime. That is also the next tool for increasing attention, so this serves double duty in helping you sleep at night and focus during the day.

Stress Management

Stress management can improve your attention. Simply stated, stress interferes with your attention, and the more you manage it, the more you have control over your own attention. Research has shown that stress negatively impacts working memory (Luethi, Meier, and Sandi 2008).

Let's quickly review two of the simplest stress management strategies: (1) mindfulness and (2) deep breathing.

Mindfulness

Mindfulness isn't about blocking out the bad, the chaotic, and the difficult. It's about acknowledging it, and then choosing how you react to it. When you are being mindful, you are more in control of your attention and your energy.

Many meditation teachers have used the metaphor of the ocean to help you understand mindfulness. Think of a boat on the high seas. On the surface, there may be storms and waves and all sorts of commotion. Without mindfulness, that is your attention. Ideas and topics and things that move and break your attention are the waves. They crash into your boat, rock it, move it, splash water into it. Your mind is all over the place. You can't manage anything.

Now, imagine if your attention is not a boat on top of the water, but a submarine deep, deep below it. The waves would cease to exist. The water would be calm and still. The crashing and twisting and churning would still be going on, but they wouldn't affect you.

TRY IT Set aside fifteen minutes to practice mindfulness. During that time, if you find yourself thinking, label it "thinking." That's the simplest way to get started. If you start to think you are not good at mindfulness, label that thought "judgment." That's it for now. The directions are easy, but the practice is not. This is just a way to start, and there are many wonderful apps out there to give you guidance. If you want to dive deeper on this tool, check out the apps Calm and Headspace.

Breathing

Many professional athletes are trained in breathing as a way of enhancing their performance. Don't be fooled by how simple this sounds; the results can be powerful. Simply put, deeper breathing is more healthy than shallow breathing. Breathing from your belly, called diaphragmatic breathing, sets off a cascade of positive health benefits. To give you an idea, shallow breathing has been associated with headaches, stomachaches, and difficulty paying attention.

The research about the effect of breathing on health and attention is well established. Its effects on health are so profound and so well replicated that it should be common sense that our breath represents our state of mind in so many ways. When we're anxious, our breath gets short, and when we're happy or relaxed, we breathe more deeply.

Here's a simple visualization to give this a whirl. Pretend you're going to blow out a birthday candle; inhale for five seconds and then extend your exhale to five seconds to blow out the candles.

There are many, many different strategies for stress management, including guided imagery and music. Set a goal to explore and experiment with some new stress management tools.

Time in Nature

Every human being desires a connection to nature, whether they know it or not. There's a reason why we sometimes need to "unplug" and go for a hike, camp out, or just take a walk around the block. Being in nature is in our instincts; it gives us a fresh start because it brings us back to our foundation.

As human beings, we were made to spend time in nature. We went from hunting and fishing to farming to creating houses and buildings and concrete jungles. We weren't designed to spend all of our days inside.

Naturalist John Muir wrote in a letter to his sisters in 1873: "The mountains are calling, and I must go." The mountains didn't physically give John Muir a call on his iPhone or send him a Snapchat. He felt connected to the mountains in a spiritual way. They revitalized him, motivating him to preserve the mountains and nature. They made him more productive in his writing, advocacy, and, most likely, many other aspects of his life.

Anything that allows you to take a step back, get outside of the box figuratively (or literally by just getting out of your box of a building or house), and disconnect from everything else going on will allow you to be more attentive when you reenter whatever you were doing before.

Research has shown that even pictures of nature or a window with a view to nature can improve attention. One study found that looking at cute pictures of puppies could increase attention, narrow focus, and promote careful behavior (Nittono et al. 2012). And if videos of cute animals can boost your attention, think of what a super boost it would be to take a walk in nature.

Happiness

Happiness increases attention and focus. One study found that students who were asked to think about a happy memory before taking a standardized math test did better than those who were not primed for happiness (Bryan and Bryan 1991).

Humor increases memory and attention. One time I had to remember to pick up Aspen animal bedding for my guinea pig, Cookie. I pictured Cookie skiing on the slopes in Aspen, Colorado, and I remembered to get the bedding. This effect suggests that educational policy should take a different attitude toward class clowns. Instead of sending them to the principal, maybe they should stand beside the teacher like a sign language expert and translate the learning material into funny jokes! Seriously, though, when you study, you could take ideas that need to be memorized and create funny unexpected visual images, like I did to remember to get bedding for Cookie.

It's not just that getting good grades will make you happy but also that being happy can get you good grades. As research studies have shown, boosting happiness can take small things, like thinking about a happy memory or allowing yourself a small treat.

TRY IT One of the most powerful tools documented to boost happiness is gratefulness. When you need a boost, take out your journal or Notes app and write about three things you are grateful for.

Dr. Lara Says

Throughout the book, you've read many examples of positive self-talk. If happiness improves attention, then we can infer that these tools will not only boost your mood but also increase your attention and performance overall. A simple way to remember this is to choose being encouraging to yourself rather than discouraging.

Talking Out Loud

Positive thinking can go a long, long way in any situation life throws at you. For those of you who get stuck in your own head, positive thinking may not be enough. That's why when you read "positive self-talk," you could actually take it literally, and talk out loud. You may think you sound crazy at first, but sometimes the crazier option is to keep your voice in your head, bottled up with all your other emotions, self-doubts, and whatever else is attempting to drag you down to the bottom of the sea of failure. When you speak out loud, you can physically hear yourself.

Talking to yourself is all good. First, it improves your selective attention. Think about it—when you are talking out loud, you can't think about anything else, so your focus is very narrow. Pro tip: Speaking your own name instead of saying "I" gives you a broader perspective; it takes you out of the I and can help limit self-criticism (Wong 2017).

If you are in a tough spot or in the middle of a dark time, talking out loud, specifically as a form of positive reinforcement or encouragement, can help your thinking process and overall mental health.

Using a Talent

In his 2018 book *The Happiness Advantage*, Shawn Achor shows that one way to boost happiness is to use a talent, skill, or character strength. He writes, "Studies have shown that the more you use your signature strengths in daily life, the happier you become." The takeaway here is that you have control over your happiness and that you can use super skill number one, finding gifts, to boost your happiness, which then boosts your attention!

TRY IT List three activities that use one of your gifts. For example, if you are a talented artist, you can (1) draw a picture on a card to give to someone, (2) hang one of your paintings on your wall, or (3) draw cheerful pictures and bring them to a children's hospital.

Interest

By definition, interest involves attention. According to *Merriam-Webster*, synonyms for "interest" include "attentiveness, undivided attention, absorption, engrossment, notice, and scrutiny." The noun definition is the state of wanting to know or learn about something or someone. You may not be interested in some of the material you are learning in American history, but what if you went to see the play *Hamilton*? You would likely be delighted because of how contemporary and wildly entertaining it is … and you would learn a lot of history.

One study asked workers to categorize their work as a job, a career, or a calling. The people who had a calling worked harder and longer, and they found their work more rewarding (Wrzesniewski et al. 1997).

Think of your attention as a jet stream, which is a scientific term for fast-flowing air currents. These currents take a plane where it's going faster and with less effort, and save on the cost of fuel. If you're flying with a jet stream, you speed up, and if you fly against it, you slow down. Any person's interest will intensify their attention.

From the beginning of your education and throughout your career, any way you can find to make something more interesting is going to increase attention. You can also apply the idea to trying to make tasks more fun or finding ways you can gamify them. For example, someone who is a coffee barista might find it hard to think about working a long shift and may not be interested in the activity, but they can choose to gamify it, or create a challenge out of it. They might create a challenge:

"I want to see how many customers I can serve today" or "I want to get so good at making drinks that I know how to make every one without looking at the ingredients list."

If you decide to take a different approach, you will gain interest in the task at hand, and therefore will most likely engage in flow, and be less distracted as a result. Starbucks hires teens at age sixteen. Starbucks also offers free tuition for Arizona State University and access to online courses. Something to think about to help save money for college!

Limiting Technology

Limiting social media is a key component to increasing your attention. Multitasking is a myth; rather than increasing productivity, it leads to taking more time to get things done and making more errors (Crenshaw 2008). If you can't limit yourself when it comes to how often or how long you look at Facebook, Instagram, or Snapchat, reconsider your options. Write a pro versus con list of each application. Are they worth it? Does the three or more hours you spend scrolling and liking and commenting and sharing every day outweigh what you would otherwise be doing? Do the pros outweigh the cons? Can you use technology responsibly?

TRY IT   Challenge yourself to limit yourself to under an hour of screen time for one day. Create a reward system for doing so. After trying this experiment, what do you notice? Write the pros and cons in your Notes app or journal, and look at it each time you feel tempted. Answer this question in the same notes page: *Why do I want to log onto Facebook (or Instagram or Snapchat)? Is it to feel connected? To stay in the loop?*

If something does distract you, ask yourself, *Can I come back to that when I finish what I am doing?* If so, jot it down. This gets the distraction off your mind and you can follow up later without getting off track.

Positive Self-Talk

When you feel distracted by social media, tell yourself, *I can take control of my phone instead of my phone taking control of me.*

Or: *I don't have to be automatic and respond to what's happening on my phone.*

Technology might be responsible for what people are calling the "crisis of cognition." These simple strategies are not the solution to the crisis of cognition, but they can help:

- Put your phone on sleep mode when you need to focus on a task.

- Turn off notifications.

- Put your phone in another room when you sleep.

You may have noticed that lots of other teens are up late, pinging you with texts all through the night. This takes us right back to the importance of sleep. Sleep is a foundation of attention, and your phone pinging you throughout the night will disrupt sleep and your ability to pay attention the next day.

When you are doing your homework, it can be as simple as putting your phone in another room and then having access to it at specified breaks. You should use time on your phone as a reward for completing a task rather than as a distraction from getting started.

You can benefit from knowing that you have control over your attention. Even if you have ADHD or executive dysfunction, these practices are ways to keep growing and know that you can find focus. Try to experiment with each of these techniques and find the ones that are the easiest for you to use and have the most effect.

CHAPTER 8

Super Skills:
The Mind Builder's
Guide to Your Brain

We are what we repeatedly do. Excellence, then, is not an act, but a habit.

—Aristotle

Whew! You made it to the final chapter. This book empowers you to regulate your own brain. Whether you have skimmed or thoroughly read through it, you have elevated your game in life. Give yourself a pat on the back. Seriously, try it now. Raise your arm, bend it at the elbow, and pat your back. Do this many times a day when you notice yourself overcoming resistance and making progress.

A mind builder is a teen who cares for their own mental health like a bodybuilder at a gym. Just as you can build physical strength, so too can you build mental strength. This book gives you six super skills to prepare you for adventures, challenges, stressors, setbacks, standardized tests, and dreaming it and doing it. Just as the cover of the book *The Hitchhiker's Guide to the Galaxy* featured in the book of the same name by Douglas Adams has the words "Don't Panic!" so too can you take this advice as you set out on your journey with confidence and calm. Let me give you a challenge: take full ownership of your life. That's the essential outcome of executive functioning. You may feel it's unfair to ask you to take ownership of your own life when you're not even an adult yet and your brain won't even finish developing until you are twenty-five. You may feel like you've been dealt a poor hand of cards with an executive dysfunction. These are justifiable complaints.

Dr. Lara Says

You cannot control the cards you are dealt, but you can control how you play the game of life. The more skills you have, the more chance you have of achieving your highest potential.

There's a chance that your challenges with executive functioning are related to your genes—for example, the gene DRD4-7R (sounds like a droid, doesn't it?) is associated with ADHD and risk taking (Eisenberg et al. 2010). The message here is that you should work with what you've got, but there are many positive sides I write about in *The Gift of ADHD* (2010) and *The ADHD Workbook for Teens* (2011). These positives include

142

creativity, empathy, intuition, exuberance, and being nature smart. Using the super skill of finding gifts, you can find your own unique gifts in addition to these. By taking ownership of your life and finding positives in your challenges, you can be prepared to take on the obstacles that life will inevitably throw your way.

Jocko Willink, a Navy Seal and author, says that discipline equals freedom (2017). Perhaps you associate the word "discipline" with being taken away from what you would rather be doing, or punished for not doing what you are supposed to. Internalizing these three words—discipline equals freedom— can free you from any negative associations. This amazing reframe suggests the opposite: that discipline allows you to get what you want.

Dr. Lara Says

It's time to think of discipline not as a burden, not only as a thing related to school but also as a pathway to freedom. You can achieve your goals despite the uncontrollable realities of nature and nurture. If you are disciplined, you can become the hero of your own journey.

When these six super skills become not just a means to achieve one goal but actual habits, think of what you are capable of doing!

Turning the Super Skills into Habits

Once you achieve your goals, you will want to keep the habits that got you to those goals. Let's say you wanted to get a good score on the SAT and used all six super skills to get that goal. The idea isn't to throw away the super skills at that point; the benefits go beyond the goal.

If you used the super skill of chunking to create a habit of studying for the SAT for one hour every Saturday morning, after you complete the SAT, you can use that habit to begin writing your essays for college. This will allow you to avoid panic the week before applications are due.

It's not about specific acts, but about how the culmination of many acts over time come together to produce a result. If you can take these super skills into days, weeks, months, and years, you can achieve your goals. You can become a more efficient, disciplined teen, able to challenge the overwhelming number of distractions you face each day. Don't quit sharpening your knife; be a lifelong learner. Build on top of your skills. The more you practice them, the easier they will become, and the faster you will be able to use them.

It takes at least two months, and sometimes up to eight months, to form a habit, but research suggests that missing a few days of practicing your habit doesn't affect the habit formation process (Lally et al. 2010). You don't have to be perfect. Just keep making progress.

Visual Reminders

What inspires you to keep going? What will you see that will make you think, *Oh, I should (should not) do this?* Post-it notes? Google Calendar? Google Tasks?

Figure out what works best for you. What will keep you motivated? Who or what will hold you accountable? As you read through the suggestions that follow, write down one action step to increase your use of visual reminders.

- **Index Cards**

  Write down your top three priorities each day on an index card. You can carry it with you as a reminder. If you have a long, overwhelming list of tasks, the process of determining the top three priorities each day will keep you on target.

- **Vision Board**

  Find images of your goals, your dreams come true. These may include schools you want to go to, fitness goals, places you want to visit, experiences you want to have—there is no limit. Print out these images from the internet or cut them out of magazines. You can even draw your own pictures. The same poster board you use for your presentations in school can be used to display your goals in vivid graphics and photos.

- **Post-it Notes**

  These are probably the most visual reminders you're going to see—at your desk, on your fridge, or even on your wall. They are front and center and in your face. You can use colorful Post-it notes of any size and colorful markers. You can use them to help with planning by writing down due dates of high-priority projects or just remembering to feed your dog. You can use them to keep motivational quotes close at hand. You can write down a compliment you received and post it in a place where you will see it often. You can write down your top three goals to help you prioritize.

Pep Talk: Keeping It Going

Imagine that you've mastered all six skills. Then what? Look at where you are, then look at where you want to go. The more you can learn about yourself, about who you are, what you do, what you like, what you don't like, what you believe in, and what you don't believe in, the better you will be able to live your life in terms of efficiency, happiness, and inspiring others. Keep the habits going. In this process, you will gain self-knowledge that will improve your ability to find direction in life.

Stay hungry. Are you going to fall off the wagon? Yes. Does that mean you have to stay off? No. Hop back on. Embrace failure. It's only through failing that we learn and adapt and become better. Habits take work. All good things come with time. You have to be willing to act daily and think yearly. It's the day in and day out grind that will produce the most results, but they won't be able to be seen immediately. You need to have faith. To trust the process.

Think about planting a fruit tree. This process starts with digging a hole, putting in a seed, covering that seed, and then returning to water it daily. There are also other factors to take into consideration, such as the quality of the soil, the need for fertilizer, the amount of sunlight, and keeping away harmful bugs or pesky critters looking for a quick meal. It's not easy to raise a tree, but with the proper habits and skills, you can achieve your goals and reap the fruits of your labor.

Your ability to apply your skills and good habits in other areas of your life will be a key factor in determining your ultimate success, so choose goals in a variety of areas. Maybe the first is school related. Maybe the next has to do with a hobby. Then it's a relationship. Think about cross-training. By mixing up your workout and exercise routines, you are likely to stay with it longer. Cross-training will allow you to build different muscle groups. So too as you build super skills across many goals, you will strengthen your self-discipline and build confidence and flexible thinking.

What You Can Control and What You Cannot

Here's a hot take on how to gain wisdom—figure out what you can control and what you cannot. You may not be able to control that you got the strictest geometry teacher, but you can control how hard you study for the class. You can control how many times you practice shooting hoops, but you can't control whether you get chosen for the varsity team. You can control how you manage your mood, but you can't control the curveballs life will throw at you.

Life is filled with bumps in the road, being dealt bad hands, and, at times, disasters. The second law of thermodynamics states that in a closed system the universe tends toward "entropy." What this essentially means is that disorder and randomness are basic givens of life. These are not "bad things happening to me" but rather predictable experiences of being human. You might wonder whether these experiences serve a function.

I think the answer is yes. Physical chemist Ilya Prigogine was awarded the Nobel Prize in Chemistry in 1977 for his discovery of dissipative structures—that is, structures that are out of balance. He found that in chaos a system will fall apart for the purpose of reorganizing at a higher level.

Dr. Lara Says

In those moments when things do fall apart, there can be opportunity. The more you can apply your super skills in chaotic times, the more you will evolve toward a higher level of functioning. Chaos can lead to a higher order. When bad things happen, find support for your grief. Don't jump over the loss or expect renewal to happen instantly. It may take time, but knowing you can find meaning at some point in the future can be a comfort in your challenges.

Positive Self-Talk

Tell yourself, *I can use the super skills to create order out of chaos.*

If you know what you can control and what you cannot, you will not waste your time, resources, and energy on things, people, and places that are not in your control in the first place. As a result, you will actually become more efficient. You will be able to direct your energy to things that truly matter, that are important to you as well as others.

It's the wisdom to know the difference that is the hardest part. What is in our control, and what's not? I don't think we'll ever be able to know 100 percent, but the more we meditate on our decisions, actions, and abilities, the more we can come to understand who we are and what we are capable of.

A Call to Action

Executive functioning includes practicing self-control to set and get your goals. It can help you realize your true capabilities and show you how far you can go. Think about how good it would feel if you worked out every day for a month, or actually sat down to study for the SAT for at least one hour every week. You build determination every time you use your inner strength.

Maybe you told yourself you wouldn't eat sugar for a month, or that you would volunteer once a week this year. As human beings, it's hard to practice willpower. Period. Regardless of the activity. Think about how many New Year's resolutions don't stick. Why is that?

Self-control, like anything else in life that you want to become good at, takes practice. And like anything else that you want to become good at, you need to do it over and over again until it becomes a habit.

It takes grit and guts to get out when you feel stuck in a negative routine, a negative habit, a negative rhythm. But keep your eye on the prize. Just as Obi-Wan Kenobi said, "Use the force, Luke," I'm telling you to use the super skills.

There is no one else out there like you. Remember that. You are unique. You have the courage and the capacity to make a difference in yourself, as well as a difference in others, either directly or indirectly. Dig deep and figure out what works for you. When you fall down or find yourself in the dumps, pick yourself back up. If you can't pick yourself back up, make sure you have a support system that is willing to give you a helping hand.

TRY IT Write a letter to yourself to open one year from now. Include:

- the three most important goals you plan to accomplish in the upcoming year,

- the three most helpful lessons you learned from reading this book,

- what you are most hopeful for, and

- what you are most worried about.

Acting as your own coach or cheerleader, add an inspirational message to yourself.

After you write the letter, put it in a safe place. Set a reminder on your smartphone for the same date one year from now with directions to open the letter and where to find it.

As human beings, we are constantly in flux. We are forever adapting to the world around us. But remember that we are also forever changing the world. It's a push-pull effect. A two-way street. A combination of our inner selves interacting with the external world. It's a balancing act that will continue for all our lives. If we fail to adapt to the world around us, we will struggle. If we fail to be unique, to be ourselves, to leave our own imprint on the world, the world will lose our gifts to it. Ultimately, finding our own gifts benefits the world we live in.

Be a Mind Builder

Before we end, I'll let you in on one more secret. These super skills can become superpowers and make you a hero. These skills will build your executive functioning. Think of body-builders: they don't simply maintain their health; they inspire others with a constant dedication to strength and fitness. If you practice the super skills like an Olympic athlete in training, you will do more than you dreamed possible and inspire others.

You can be a mind builder. You can encourage yourself and others like Oprah Winfrey, plan and strategize like former president Dwight D. Eisenhower, get results one step at a time like astronaut Neil Armstrong, be motivating through hard times like poet Maya Angelou, stay calm in chaos like a Zen monk, and focus like chess Grandmaster Maurice Ashley.

When you set a goal, you aren't just patching up weak-nesses, you are setting out on a hero's journey. You will depart from your ordinary world, confront crises, overcome ordeals, and then return to your starting place transformed. It is in the depths of being tested that you will forge your determination.

You're the owner of your brain, but it goes deeper than that. You're the owner of the "you." There isn't another you. There never has been and never will be. Relish that. Cherish it. Use it as motivation to become whatever it is you want to become.

References and Resources

Achor, S. 2018. *The Happiness Advantage: The Seven Principles of Positive Psychology That Fuel Success and Performance at Work.* New York: Currency.

Bandura, A. 1997. *Self-Efficacy: The Exercise of Control.* Stanford, CA: W. H. Freeman & Company.

Barrett, L. G. 2017. *How Emotions Are Made: The Secret Life of the Brain.* New York: Houghton Mifflin Harcourt.

Ben-Shahar, T. 2007. *Happier: Learn the Secrets to Daily Joy and Lasting Fulfillment.* 1st ed. New York: McGraw-Hill Education.

Bryan, T., and J. Bryan. 1991. "Positive Mood and Math Performance." *Journal of Learning Disabilities* 24: 490–494.

Burnett, J. 2018. "Survey: 42 Percent of American Teenagers Feel Anxious When Away From Their Cell Phones." The Ladders. https://www.theladders.com/career-advice/survey-42-of-american-teengers-feel-anxious-when-away-from-their-cell-phones.

Carlson, K. A. 2011 "The Impact of Humor on Memory: Is the Humor Effect About Humor?" *Psychology Faculty Publications* 21. https://scholar.valpo.edu/psych_fac_pub/21.

Crenshaw, D. 2008. *The Myth of Multitasking: How "Doing It All" Gets Nothing Done.* San Francisco: Jossey-Bass.

Danielson, M. L., R. H. Bitsko, R. M. Ghandour, J. R. Holbrook, M. D. Kogan, and S. Blumberg. 2018. "Prevalence of Parent-Reported ADHD Diagnosis and Associated Treatment Among U.S. Children and Adolescents, 2016." *Journal of Clinical Child and Adolescent Psychology* 47(2): 199–212.

Deak, J., and T. Deak. 2013. *The Owner's Manual for Driving Your Adolescent Brain.* Naperville, IL: Little Pickle Press.

Duckworth, A. L., and M. E. P. Seligman. 2005. "Self-Discipline Outdoes IQ in Predicting Academic Performance in Adolescents." *Psychological Science* 16(12): 939–944.

Dweck, C. S. 2007. *Mindset: The New Psychology of Success.* New York: Ballantine Books.

Eisenberg, D. T., C. L. Apicella, B. C. Campbell, A. Dreber, J. R. Garcia, and J. K. Lum. 2010. "Assortative Human Pair-Bonding for Partner Ancestry and Allelic Variation of the Dopamine Receptor D4 (Drd4) Gene." *Social Cognitive and Affective Neuroscience* 5(2–3): 194–202.

Gazzaley, A. 2018. "The Cognition Crisis." https://medium.com/s/futurehuman/the-cognition-crisis-a1482e889fcb.

Godman, H. 2018. "Regular Exercise Changes the Brain to Improve Memory, Thinking Skills." *Harvard Health Blog.* Accessed July 27, 2018. www.health.harvard.edu/blog /regularexercise-changes-brain-improve-memory-thinking -skills-201404097110.

Hartanto, T. A., C. E. Krafft, A. M. Iosif, and J. B. Schweitzer. 2016. "A Trial-by-Trial Analysis Reveals More Intense Physical Activity Is Associated with Better Cognitive Control Performance in Attention-Deficit/Hyperactivity Disorder." *Child Neuropsychology: A Journal on Normal and Abnormal Development in Childhood and Adolescence* 22(5): 618–626.

Hartmann, T. 2015. *ADHD and the Edison Gene: A Drug-Free Approach to Managing the Unique Qualities of Your Child.* 3rd ed. Rochester, VT: Park Street Press.

Harvard Medical School Division of Sleep Medicine. 2007. "Sleep, Performance, and Public Safety." http://healthysleep .med.harvard.edu/healthy/matters/consequences/sleep -performance-and-public-safety.

Honos-Webb, L. 2011. *The ADHD Workbook for Teens: Activities to Help You Gain Motivation and Confidence.* Oakland, CA: New Harbinger Publications.

Honos-Webb, L. 2010. *The Gift of ADHD.* 2nd ed. Oakland, CA: New Harbinger Publications.

Honos-Webb, L. 2008. *The Gift of Adult ADD*. Oakland, CA: New Harbinger Publications.

Howell, D., L. Osternig, P. Van Donkelaar, U. Mayr, and L. Chou. 2013. "Effects of Concussion on Attention and Executive Function in Adolescents." *Medicine & Science in Sports & Exercise* 45(6): 1030–37.

Hoza, B., A. L. Smith, E. K. Shoulberg, K. S. Linnea, T. E. Dorsch, J. A. Blazo, C. M. Alerding, and G. P. McCabe. 2015. "A Randomized Trial Examining the Effects of Aerobic Physical Activity on Attention-Deficit/Hyperactivity Disorder Symptoms in Young Children." *Journal of Abnormal Child Psychology* 43(4): 655–67.

Johnson, S. 2010. "Suppressing Emotions: How Shutting Down Your Feelings Can Be Disastrous to Your Relationship." https://www.psychologytoday.com/us/blog/hold-me-tight/201004/suppressing-emotions.

Kashdan, T. B., P. Ferssizidis, R. L. Collins, and M. Muraven. 2010. "Emotion Differentiation as Resilience Against Excessive Alcohol Use: An Ecological Momentary Assessment in Underage Social Drinkers." *Psychological Science* 21(9): 1341–1347.

Lally, P., C. H. van Jaarsveld, H. W. Potts, and J. Wardle. 2010. "How Are Habits Formed: Modelling Habit Formation in the Real World." *European Journal of Social Psychology* 40: 998–1009.

Levitin, D. J. 2015. *The Organized Mind: Thinking Straight in the Age of Information Overload.* New York: Penguin Random House.

Liu, C. H., C. Stevens, S. H. M. Wong, M. Yasui, and J. A. Chen. 2019. "The Prevalence and Predictors of Mental Health Diagnoses and Suicide Among U.S. College Students: Implications for Addressing Disparities in Service Use." *Depression and Anxiety* 36(1): 8–17.

Locke, E. A, and G. P. Latham. 2002. "Building a Practically Useful Theory of Goal Setting and Task Motivation: A 35-Year Odyssey." *American Psychologist* 57(9): 705–717.

Luethi, M., B. Meier, and C. Sandi. 2008. "Stress Effects on Working Memory, Explicit Memory, and Implicit Memory for Neutral and Emotional Stimuli in Healthy Men." *Frontiers in Behavioral Neuroscience* 2: 5.

Matthews, G. 2007. "The Impact of Commitment, Accountability, and Written Goals on Goal Achievement." Paper presented at the 87th Convention of the Western Psychological Association, Vancouver, BC, Canada.

Miller, W. R., and S. Rollnick. 2012. *Motivational Interviewing: Helping People Change.* 3rd ed. New York: Guilford Press.

Mobbs, D., C. C. Hagan, T. Dalgleish, B. Silston, and C. Prévost. 2015. "The Ecology of Human Fear: Survival Optimization and the Nervous System." *Frontiers in Neuroscience* 9: 55.

National Scientific Council on the Developing Child. 2005/2014. "Excessive Stress Disrupts the Architecture of the Developing Brain." Working Paper No. 3. Updated edition. Retrieved from www.developingchild.harvard.edu.

Nittono, H., M. Fukushima, A. Yano, and H. Moriya. 2012. "The Power of *Kawaii*: Viewing Cute Images Promotes a Careful Behavior and Narrows Attentional Focus." *PloS One* 7, (9): e46362.

Pink, D. H. 2009. *Drive: The Surprising Truth About What Motivates Us.* New York: Riverhead Books.

Pink, D. H. 2018. *When: The Scientific Secrets of Perfect Timing.* New York: Riverhead Books.

Ratey, J. J., with E. Hagerman. 2013. *Spark: The Revolutionary New Science of Exercise and the Brain.* Boston: Little, Brown and Company.

Ratey, J. J. "Shrink on the Move, Always Moving." TEDxManhattan Beach. Accessed July 26, 2018. tedxmanhattanbeach.com /past-events/october-2012-conference-journey-topurpose /presenters/john-ratey.

Rideout, V., and M. B. Robb. 2019. "The Common Sense Census: Media Use by Tweens and Teens." San Francisco Common Sense Media.

Sohn, S., P., B. Rees, N. J. Wildridge, and B. Carter. 2019. "Prevalence of Problematic Smartphone Usage and

Associated Mental Health Outcomes Amongst Children and Young People: A Systematic Review, Meta-Analysis and GRADE of the Evidence." *BMC Psychiatry* 19: 356.

Stiglic, N., and R. M. Viner. 2019. "Effects of Screentime on the Health and Well-being of Children and Adolescents: A Systematic Review of Reviews." *BMJ Open* 9: e023191.

Swider, B., D. Harari, A. P. Breidenthal, and L. B. Steed. 2018. "The Pros and Cons of Perfectionism." *Harvard Business Review*, December 27.

SWNS. 2017. "Americans Check Their Phones 80 Times a Day: Study." *New York Post*, November 8. Accessed July 23, 2018.

Terry, S. 2011. *100 Things: What's on Your List?* Australia: Random House.

Tracy, B. 2017. *Eat That Frog!: 21 Great Ways to Stop Procrastinating and Get More Done in Less Time*. Oakland, CA: Berrett-Koehler Publishers.

Ward, A. F., K. Duke, A. Gneezy, and M. W. Bos. 2017. "Brain Drain: The Mere Presence of One's Own Smartphone Reduces Available Cognitive Capacity." *Journal of the Association for Consumer Research* 2(2): 14–54.

White, H. 2019. "The Creativity of ADHD." *Scientific American*, March 5.

Willink, J. 2017. *Discipline Equals Freedom: Field Manual*. New York: St. Martin's Press.

Wong, K. 2017. "The Benefits of Talking to Yourself." *New York Times*, June 8.

Wrzesniewski, A., C. McCauley, P. Rozin, and B. Schwartz. 1997. "Jobs, Careers, and Callings: People's Relations to Their Work." *Journal of Research in Personality* 31(1): 21–33.

Lara Honos-Webb, PhD, is a worldwide attention deficit/hyperactivity disorder (ADHD) expert, and offers ADHD coaching. She is a clinical psychologist, and author of *The Gift of ADHD*, *The Gift of ADHD Activity Book*, *The Gift of Adult ADD*, *The ADHD Workbook for Teens*, and *Listening to Depression*. She has also published more than twenty-five scholarly articles. Learn more about her work at www.addisagift.com.

Foreword writer **Neil D. Brown, LCSW**, is author of *Ending The Parent-Teen Control Battle* and host of the *Healthy Family Connections Podcast*. Brown is a therapist, speaker, trainer, and behavioral health consultant. Learn more about his work at www.neildbrown.com.

More ⏱Instant Help Books for Teens
An Imprint of New Harbinger Publications